© 2014 by Law School Admission Council, Inc.

ISBN-13: 978-0-9860455-4-7

Print number
10 9 8 7 6 5 4 3 2 1

TABLE OF CONTENTS

INTRODUCTION TO THE LSAT

The Law School Admission Test is a half-day standardized test required for admission to all ABA-approved law schools, most Canadian law schools, and many other law schools. It consists of five 35-minute sections of multiple-choice questions. Four of the five sections contribute to the test taker's score. These sections include one Reading Comprehension section, one Analytical Reasoning section, and two Logical Reasoning sections. The unscored section, commonly referred to as the variable section, typically is used to pretest new test questions or to preequate new test forms. The placement of this section in the LSAT will vary. A 35-minute writing sample is administered at the end of the test. The writing sample is not scored by LSAC, but copies are sent to all law schools to which you apply. The score scale for the LSAT is 120 to 180.

The LSAT is designed to measure skills considered essential for success in law school: the reading and comprehension of complex texts with accuracy and insight; the organization and management of information and the ability to draw reasonable inferences from it; the ability to think critically; and the analysis and evaluation of the reasoning and arguments of others.

The LSAT provides a standard measure of acquired reading and verbal reasoning skills that law schools can use as one of several factors in assessing applicants.

For up-to-date information about LSAC's services, go to our website, LSAC.org.

SCORING

Your LSAT score is based on the number of questions you answer correctly (the raw score). There is no deduction for incorrect answers, and all questions count equally. In other words, there is no penalty for guessing.

Test Score Accuracy—Reliability and Standard Error of Measurement

Candidates perform at different levels on different occasions for reasons quite unrelated to the characteristics of a test itself. The accuracy of test scores is best described by the use of two related statistical terms: reliability and standard error of measurement.

Reliability is a measure of how consistently a test measures the skills being assessed. The higher the reliability coefficient for a test, the more certain we can be that test takers would get very similar scores if they took the test again.

LSAC reports an internal consistency measure of reliability for every test form. Reliability can vary from 0.00 to 1.00, and a test with no measurement error would have a reliability coefficient of 1.00 (never attained in practice). Reliability

coefficients for past LSAT forms have ranged from .90 to .95, indicating a high degree of consistency for these tests. LSAC expects the reliability of the LSAT to continue to fall within the same range.

LSAC also reports the amount of measurement error associated with each test form, a concept known as the standard error of measurement (SEM). The SEM, which is usually about 2.6 points, indicates how close a test taker's observed score is likely to be to his or her true score. True scores are theoretical scores that would be obtained from perfectly reliable tests with no measurement error—scores never known in practice.

Score bands, or ranges of scores that contain a test taker's true score a certain percentage of the time, can be derived using the SEM. LSAT score bands are constructed by adding and subtracting the (rounded) SEM to and from an actual LSAT score (e.g., the LSAT score, plus or minus 3 points). Scores near 120 or 180 have asymmetrical bands. Score bands constructed in this manner will contain an individual's true score approximately 68 percent of the time.

Measurement error also must be taken into account when comparing LSAT scores of two test takers. It is likely that small differences in scores are due to measurement error rather than to meaningful differences in ability. The standard error of score differences provides some guidance as to the importance of differences between two scores. The standard error of score differences is approximately 1.4 times larger than the standard error of measurement for the individual scores.

Thus, a test score should be regarded as a useful but approximate measure of a test taker's abilities as measured by the test, not as an exact determination of his or her abilities. LSAC encourages law schools to examine the range of scores within the interval that probably contains the test taker's true score (e.g., the test taker's score band) rather than solely interpret the reported score alone.

Adjustments for Variation in Test Difficulty

All test forms of the LSAT reported on the same score scale are designed to measure the same abilities, but one test form may be slightly easier or more difficult than another. The scores from different test forms are made comparable through a statistical procedure known as equating. As a result of equating, a given scaled score earned on different test forms reflects the same level of ability.

Research on the LSAT

Summaries of LSAT validity studies and other LSAT research can be found in member law school libraries and at LSAC.org.

To Inquire About Test Questions

If you find what you believe to be an error or ambiguity in a test question that affects your response to the question, contact LSAC by e-mail: LSATTS@LSAC.org, or write to Law School Admission Council, Test Development Group, PO Box 40, Newtown, PA 18940-0040.

HOW THIS PREPTEST DIFFERS FROM AN ACTUAL LSAT

This PrepTest is made up of the scored sections and writing sample from the actual disclosed LSAT administered in December 2014. However, it does not contain the extra, variable section that is used to pretest new test items of one of the three multiple-choice question types. The three multiple-choice question types may be in a different order in an actual LSAT than in this PrepTest. This is because the order of these question types is intentionally varied for each administration of the test.

THE THREE LSAT MULTIPLE-CHOICE QUESTION TYPES

The multiple-choice questions that make up most of the LSAT reflect a broad range of academic disciplines and are intended to give no advantage to candidates from a particular academic background.

The five sections of the test contain three different question types. The following material presents a general discussion of the nature of each question type and some strategies that can be used in answering them.

Analytical Reasoning Questions

Analytical Reasoning questions are designed to assess the ability to consider a group of facts and rules, and, given those facts and rules, determine what could or must be true. The specific scenarios associated with these questions are usually unrelated to law, since they are intended to be accessible to a wide range of test takers. However, the skills tested parallel those involved in determining what could or must be the case given a set of regulations, the terms of a contract, or the facts of a legal case in relation to the law. In Analytical Reasoning questions, you are asked to reason deductively from a set of statements and rules or principles that describe relationships among persons, things, or events.

Analytical Reasoning questions appear in sets, with each set based on a single passage. The passage used for each set of questions describes common ordering relationships or grouping relationships, or a combination of both types of relationships. Examples include scheduling employees for work shifts, assigning instructors to class sections,

ordering tasks according to priority, and distributing grants for projects.

Analytical Reasoning questions test a range of deductive reasoning skills. These include:

- Comprehending the basic structure of a set of relationships by determining a complete solution to the problem posed (for example, an acceptable seating arrangement of all six diplomats around a table)

- Reasoning with conditional ("if-then") statements and recognizing logically equivalent formulations of such statements

- Inferring what could be true or must be true from given facts and rules

- Inferring what could be true or must be true from given facts and rules together with new information in the form of an additional or substitute fact or rule

- Recognizing when two statements are logically equivalent in context by identifying a condition or rule that could replace one of the original conditions while still resulting in the same possible outcomes

Analytical Reasoning questions reflect the kinds of detailed analyses of relationships and sets of constraints that a law student must perform in legal problem solving. For example, an Analytical Reasoning passage might describe six diplomats being seated around a table, following certain rules of protocol as to who can sit where. You, the test taker, must answer questions about the logical implications of given and new information. For example, you may be asked who can sit between diplomats X and Y, or who cannot sit next to X if W sits next to Y. Similarly, if you were a student in law school, you might be asked to analyze a scenario involving a set of particular circumstances and a set of governing rules in the form of constitutional provisions, statutes, administrative codes, or prior rulings that have been upheld. You might then be asked to determine the legal options in the scenario: what is required given the scenario, what is permissible given the scenario, and what is prohibited given the scenario. Or you might be asked to develop a "theory" for the case: when faced with an incomplete set of facts about the case, you must fill in the picture based on what is implied by the facts that are known. The problem could be elaborated by the addition of new information or hypotheticals.

No formal training in logic is required to answer these questions correctly. Analytical Reasoning questions are intended to be answered using knowledge, skills, and reasoning ability generally expected of college students and graduates.

Suggested Approach

Some people may prefer to answer first those questions about a passage that seem less difficult and then those that seem more difficult. In general, it is best to finish one passage before starting on another, because much time can be lost in returning to a passage and reestablishing familiarity with its relationships. However, if you are having great difficulty on one particular set of questions and are spending too much time on them, it may be to your advantage to skip that set of questions and go on to the next passage, returning to the problematic set of questions after you have finished the other questions in the section.

Do not assume that because the conditions for a set of questions look long or complicated, the questions based on those conditions will be especially difficult.

Read the passage carefully. Careful reading and analysis are necessary to determine the exact nature of the relationships involved in an Analytical Reasoning passage. Some relationships are fixed (for example, P and R must always work on the same project). Other relationships are variable (for example, Q must be assigned to either team 1 or team 3). Some relationships that are not stated explicitly in the conditions are implied by and can be deduced from those that are stated (for example, if one condition about paintings in a display specifies that Painting K must be to the left of Painting Y, and another specifies that Painting W must be to the left of Painting K, then it can be deduced that Painting W must be to the left of Painting Y).

In reading the conditions, do not introduce unwarranted assumptions. For instance, in a set of questions establishing relationships of height and weight among the members of a team, do not assume that a person who is taller than another person must weigh more than that person. As another example, suppose a set involves ordering and a question in the set asks what must be true if both X and Y must be earlier than Z; in this case, do not assume that X must be earlier than Y merely because X is mentioned before Y. All the information needed to answer each question is provided in the passage and the question itself.

The conditions are designed to be as clear as possible. Do not interpret the conditions as if they were intended to trick you. For example, if a question asks how many people could be eligible to serve on a committee, consider only those people named in the passage unless directed otherwise. When in doubt, read the conditions in their most obvious sense. Remember, however, that the language in the conditions is intended to be read for precise meaning. It is essential to pay particular attention to words that describe or limit relationships, such as "only," "exactly," "never," "always," "must be," "cannot be," and the like.

The result of this careful reading will be a clear picture of the structure of the relationships involved, including the kinds of relationships permitted, the participants in the relationships, and the range of possible actions or attributes for these participants.

Keep in mind question independence. Each question should be considered separately from the other questions in its set. No information, except what is given in the original conditions, should be carried over from one question to another.

In some cases a question will simply ask for conclusions to be drawn from the conditions as originally given. Some questions may, however, add information to the original conditions or temporarily suspend or replace one of the original conditions for the purpose of that question only. For example, if Question 1 adds the supposition "if P is sitting at table 2 …," this supposition should NOT be carried over to any other question in the set.

Consider highlighting text and using diagrams. Many people find it useful to underline key points in the passage and in each question. In addition, it may prove very helpful to draw a diagram to assist you in finding the solution to the problem.

In preparing for the test, you may wish to experiment with different types of diagrams. For a scheduling problem, a simple calendar-like diagram may be helpful. For a grouping problem, an array of labeled columns or rows may be useful.

Even though most people find diagrams to be very helpful, some people seldom use them, and for some individual questions no one will need a diagram. There is by no means universal agreement on which kind of diagram is best for which problem or in which cases a diagram is most useful. Do not be concerned if a particular problem in the test seems to be best approached without the use of a diagram.

Logical Reasoning Questions

Arguments are a fundamental part of the law, and analyzing arguments is a key element of legal analysis. Training in the law builds on a foundation of basic reasoning skills. Law students must draw on the skills of analyzing, evaluating, constructing, and refuting arguments. They need to be able to identify what information is relevant to an issue or argument and what impact further evidence might have. They need to be able to reconcile opposing positions and use arguments to persuade others.

Logical Reasoning questions evaluate the ability to analyze, critically evaluate, and complete arguments as they occur in ordinary language. The questions are based on short arguments drawn from a wide variety of sources, including newspapers, general interest magazines, scholarly publications, advertisements, and informal discourse. These arguments mirror legal reasoning in the types of arguments presented and in their complexity, though few of the arguments actually have law as a subject matter.

Each Logical Reasoning question requires you to read and comprehend a short passage, then answer one question (or, rarely, two questions) about it. The questions are designed to assess a wide range of skills involved in thinking critically, with an emphasis on skills that are central to legal reasoning.

These skills include:

- Recognizing the parts of an argument and their relationships

- Recognizing similarities and differences between patterns of reasoning

- Drawing well-supported conclusions

- Reasoning by analogy

- Recognizing misunderstandings or points of disagreement

- Determining how additional evidence affects an argument

- Detecting assumptions made by particular arguments

- Identifying and applying principles or rules

- Identifying flaws in arguments

- Identifying explanations

The questions do not presuppose specialized knowledge of logical terminology. For example, you will not be expected to know the meaning of specialized terms such as "ad hominem" or "syllogism." On the other hand, you will be expected to understand and critique the reasoning contained in arguments. This requires that you possess a university-level understanding of widely used concepts such as argument, premise, assumption, and conclusion.

Suggested Approach

Read each question carefully. Make sure that you understand the meaning of each part of the question. Make sure that you understand the meaning of each answer choice and the ways in which it may or may not relate to the question posed.

Do not pick a response simply because it is a true statement. Although true, it may not answer the question posed.

Answer each question on the basis of the information that is given, even if you do not agree with it. Work within the context provided by the passage. LSAT questions do not involve any tricks or hidden meanings.

Reading Comprehension Questions

Both law school and the practice of law revolve around extensive reading of highly varied, dense, argumentative, and expository texts (for example, cases, codes, contracts, briefs, decisions, evidence). This reading must be exacting, distinguishing precisely what is said from what is not said. It involves comparison, analysis, synthesis, and application (for example, of principles and rules). It involves drawing appropriate inferences and applying ideas and arguments to new contexts. Law school reading also requires the ability to grasp unfamiliar subject matter and the ability to penetrate difficult and challenging material.

The purpose of LSAT Reading Comprehension questions is to measure the ability to read, with understanding and insight, examples of lengthy and complex materials similar to those commonly encountered in law school. The Reading Comprehension section of the LSAT contains four sets of reading questions, each set consisting of a selection of reading material followed by five to eight questions. The reading selection in three of the four sets consists of a single reading passage; the other set contains two related shorter passages. Sets with two passages are a variant of Reading Comprehension called Comparative Reading, which was introduced in June 2007.

Comparative Reading questions concern the relationships between the two passages, such as those of generalization/instance, principle/application, or point/counterpoint. Law school work often requires reading two or more texts in conjunction with each other and understanding their relationships. For example, a law student may read a trial court decision together with an appellate court decision that overturns it, or identify the fact pattern from a hypothetical suit together with the potentially controlling case law.

Reading selections for LSAT Reading Comprehension questions are drawn from a wide range of subjects in the humanities, the social sciences, the biological and physical sciences, and areas related to the law. Generally, the selections are densely written, use high-level vocabulary, and contain sophisticated argument or complex rhetorical structure (for example, multiple points of view). Reading Comprehension questions require you to read carefully and accurately, to determine the relationships among the various parts of the reading selection, and to draw reasonable inferences from the material in the selection. The questions may ask about the following characteristics of a passage or pair of passages:

- The main idea or primary purpose

- Information that is explicitly stated

- Information or ideas that can be inferred

- The meaning or purpose of words or phrases as used in context

- The organization or structure

- The application of information in the selection to a new context

- Principles that function in the selection

- Analogies to claims or arguments in the selection

- An author's attitude as revealed in the tone of a passage or the language used

- The impact of new information on claims or arguments in the selection

Suggested Approach

Since reading selections are drawn from many different disciplines and sources, you should not be discouraged if you encounter material with which you are not familiar. It is important to remember that questions are to be answered exclusively on the basis of the information provided in the selection. There is no particular knowledge that you are expected to bring to the test, and you should not make inferences based on any prior knowledge of a subject that you may have. You may, however, wish to defer working on a set of questions that seems particularly difficult or unfamiliar until after you have dealt with sets you find easier.

Strategies. One question that often arises in connection with Reading Comprehension has to do with the most effective and efficient order in which to read the selections and questions. Possible approaches include:

- reading the selection very closely and then answering the questions;

- reading the questions first, reading the selection closely, and then returning to the questions; or

- skimming the selection and questions very quickly, then rereading the selection closely and answering the questions.

Test takers are different, and the best strategy for one might not be the best strategy for another. In preparing for the test, therefore, you might want to experiment with the different strategies and decide what works most effectively for you.

Remember that your strategy must be effective under timed conditions. For this reason, the first strategy—reading the selection very closely and then answering the questions—may be the most effective for you. Nonetheless, if you believe that one of the other strategies

might be more effective for you, you should try it out and assess your performance using it.

Reading the selection. Whatever strategy you choose, you should give the passage or pair of passages at least one careful reading before answering the questions. Try to distinguish main ideas from supporting ideas, and opinions or attitudes from factual, objective information. Note transitions from one idea to the next and identify the relationships among the different ideas or parts of a passage, or between the two passages in Comparative Reading sets. Consider how and why an author makes points and draws conclusions. Be sensitive to implications of what the passages say.

You may find it helpful to mark key parts of passages. For example, you might underline main ideas or important arguments, and you might circle transitional words—"although," "nevertheless," "correspondingly," and the like—that will help you map the structure of a passage. Also, you might note descriptive words that will help you identify an author's attitude toward a particular idea or person.

Answering the Questions

- Always read all the answer choices before selecting the best answer. The best answer choice is the one that most accurately and completely answers the question being posed.

- Respond to the specific question being asked. Do not pick an answer choice simply because it is a true statement. For example, picking a true statement might yield an incorrect answer to a question in which you are asked to identify an author's position on an issue, since you are not being asked to evaluate the truth of the author's position but only to correctly identify what that position is.

- Answer the questions only on the basis of the information provided in the selection. Your own views, interpretations, or opinions, and those you have heard from others, may sometimes conflict with those expressed in a reading selection; however, you are expected to work within the context provided by the reading selection. You should not expect to agree with everything you encounter in Reading Comprehension passages.

THE WRITING SAMPLE

On the day of the test, you will be asked to write one sample essay. LSAC does not score the writing sample, but copies are sent to all law schools to which you apply. According to a 2006 LSAC survey of 157 United States and Canadian law schools, almost all use the writing sample in evaluating at least some applications for admission. Failure to respond to writing sample prompts and frivolous responses have been used by law schools as grounds for rejection of applications for admission.

In developing and implementing the writing sample portion of the LSAT, LSAC has operated on the following premises: First, law schools and the legal profession value highly the ability to communicate effectively in writing. Second, it is important to encourage potential law students to develop effective writing skills. Third, a sample of an applicant's writing, produced under controlled conditions, is a potentially useful indication of that person's writing ability. Fourth, the writing sample can serve as an independent check on other writing submitted by applicants as part of the admission process. Finally, writing samples may be useful for diagnostic purposes related to improving a candidate's writing.

The writing prompt presents a decision problem. You are asked to make a choice between two positions or courses of action. Both of the choices are defensible, and you are given criteria and facts on which to base your decision. There is no "right" or "wrong" position to take on the topic, so the quality of each test taker's response is a function not of which choice is made, but of how well or poorly the choice is supported and how well or poorly the other choice is criticized.

The LSAT writing prompt was designed and validated by legal education professionals. Since it involves writing based on fact sets and criteria, the writing sample gives applicants the opportunity to demonstrate the type of argumentative writing that is required in law school, although the topics are usually nonlegal.

You will have 35 minutes in which to plan and write an essay on the topic you receive. Read the topic and the accompanying directions carefully. You will probably find it best to spend a few minutes considering the topic and organizing your thoughts before you begin writing. In your essay, be sure to develop your ideas fully, leaving time, if possible, to review what you have written. Do not write on a topic other than the one specified. Writing on a topic of your own choice is not acceptable.

No special knowledge is required or expected for this writing exercise. Law schools are interested in the reasoning, clarity, organization, language usage, and writing mechanics displayed in your essay. How well you write is more important than how much you write. Confine your essay to the blocked, lined area on the front and back of the separate Writing Sample Response Sheet. Only that area will be reproduced for law schools. Be sure that your writing is legible.

TAKING THE PREPTEST UNDER SIMULATED LSAT CONDITIONS

One important way to prepare for the LSAT is to simulate the day of the test by taking a practice test under actual time constraints. Taking a practice test under timed conditions helps you to estimate the amount of time you can afford to spend on each question in a section and to determine the question types on which you may need additional practice.

Since the LSAT is a timed test, it is important to use your allotted time wisely. During the test, you may work only on the section designated by the test supervisor. You cannot devote extra time to a difficult section and make up that time on a section you find easier. In pacing yourself, and checking your answers, you should think of each section of the test as a separate minitest.

Be sure that you answer every question on the test. When you do not know the correct answer to a question, first eliminate the responses that you know are incorrect, then make your best guess among the remaining choices. Do not be afraid to guess as there is no penalty for incorrect answers.

When you take a practice test, abide by all the requirements specified in the directions and keep strictly within the specified time limits. Work without a rest period. When you take an actual test, you will have only a short break—usually 10–15 minutes—after SECTION III.

When taken under conditions as much like actual testing conditions as possible, a practice test provides very useful preparation for taking the LSAT.

Official directions for the four multiple-choice sections and the writing sample are included in this PrepTest so that you can approximate actual testing conditions as you practice.

To take the test:

- Set a timer for 35 minutes. Answer all the questions in SECTION I of this PrepTest. Stop working on that section when the 35 minutes have elapsed.

- Repeat, allowing yourself 35 minutes each for sections II, III, and IV.

- Set the timer again for 35 minutes, then prepare your response to the writing sample topic at the end of this PrepTest.

- Refer to "Computing Your Score" for the PrepTest for instruction on evaluating your performance. An answer key is provided for that purpose.

The practice test that follows consists of four sections corresponding to the four scored sections of the December 2014 LSAT. Also reprinted is the December 2014 unscored writing sample topic.

General Directions for the LSAT Answer Sheet

The actual testing time for this portion of the test will be 2 hours 55 minutes. There are five sections, each with a time limit of 35 minutes. The supervisor will tell you when to begin and end each section. If you finish a section before time is called, you may check your work on that section **only;** do not turn to any other section of the test book and do not work on any other section either in the test book or on the answer sheet.

There are several different types of questions on the test, and each question type has its own directions. **Be sure you understand the directions for each question type before attempting to answer any questions in that section.**

Not everyone will finish all the questions in the time allowed. Do not hurry, but work steadily and as quickly as you can without sacrificing accuracy. You are advised to use your time effectively. If a question seems too difficult, go on to the next one and return to the difficult question after completing the section. **MARK THE BEST ANSWER YOU CAN FOR EVERY QUESTION. NO DEDUCTIONS WILL BE MADE FOR WRONG ANSWERS. YOUR SCORE WILL BE BASED ONLY ON THE NUMBER OF QUESTIONS YOU ANSWER CORRECTLY.**

ALL YOUR ANSWERS MUST BE MARKED ON THE ANSWER SHEET. Answer spaces for each question are lettered to correspond with the letters of the potential answers to each question in the test book. After you have decided which of the answers is correct, blacken the corresponding space on the answer sheet. **BE SURE THAT EACH MARK IS BLACK AND COMPLETELY FILLS THE ANSWER SPACE.** Give only one answer to each question. If you change an answer, be sure that all previous marks are **erased completely.** Since the answer sheet is machine scored, incomplete erasures may be interpreted as intended answers. **ANSWERS RECORDED IN THE TEST BOOK WILL NOT BE SCORED.**

There may be more question numbers on this answer sheet than there are questions in a section. Do not be concerned, but be certain that the section and number of the question you are answering matches the answer sheet section and question number. Additional answer spaces in any answer sheet section should be left blank. Begin your next section in the number one answer space for that section.

LSAC takes various steps to ensure that answer sheets are returned from test centers in a timely manner for processing. In the unlikely event that an answer sheet is not received, LSAC will permit the examinee either to retest at no additional fee or to receive a refund of his or her LSAT fee. **THESE REMEDIES ARE THE ONLY REMEDIES AVAILABLE IN THE UNLIKELY EVENT THAT AN ANSWER SHEET IS NOT RECEIVED BY LSAC.**

Score Cancellation

Complete this section only if you are absolutely certain you want to cancel your score. **A CANCELLATION REQUEST CANNOT BE RESCINDED. IF YOU ARE AT ALL UNCERTAIN, YOU SHOULD NOT COMPLETE THIS SECTION.**

To cancel your score from this administration, you **must:**

A. fill in both ovals here ...... ◯ ◯
        AND

B. read the following statement. Then sign your name and enter the date. **YOUR SIGNATURE ALONE IS NOT SUFFICIENT FOR SCORE CANCELLATION. BOTH OVALS ABOVE MUST BE FILLED IN FOR SCANNING EQUIPMENT TO RECOGNIZE YOUR REQUEST FOR SCORE CANCELLATION.**

I certify that I wish to cancel my test score from this administration. I understand that my request is irreversible and that my score will not be sent to me or to the law schools to which I apply.

Sign your name in full

Date

FOR LSAC USE ONLY

HOW DID YOU PREPARE FOR THE LSAT?
(Select all that apply.)

Responses to this item are voluntary and will be used for statistical research purposes only.

- ◯ By studying the free sample questions available on LSAC's website.
- ◯ By taking the free sample LSAT available on LSAC's website.
- ◯ By working through official LSAT *PrepTests*, *ItemWise*, and/or other LSAC test prep products.
- ◯ By using LSAT prep books or software **not** published by LSAC.
- ◯ By attending a commercial test preparation or coaching course.
- ◯ By attending a test preparation or coaching course offered through an undergraduate institution.
- ◯ Self study.
- ◯ Other preparation.
- ◯ No preparation.

CERTIFYING STATEMENT

Please write the following statement. Sign and date.

I certify that I am the examinee whose name appears on this answer sheet and that I am here to take the LSAT for the sole purpose of being considered for admission to law school. I further certify that I will neither assist nor receive assistance from any other candidate, and I agree not to copy, retain, or transmit examination questions in any form or discuss them with any other person.

SIGNATURE: _____ TODAY'S DATE: _____ / _____ / _____
                                                   MONTH DAY YEAR

INSTRUCTIONS FOR COMPLETING THE BIOGRAPHICAL AREA ARE ON THE BACK COVER OF YOUR TEST BOOKLET.
USE ONLY A NO. 2 OR HB PENCIL TO COMPLETE THIS ANSWER SHEET. DO NOT USE INK.

A

1 LAST NAME | **FIRST NAME** | **MI**

(Grid of bubbles A–Z for each letter column)

2 LAST 4 DIGITS OF SOCIAL SECURITY / SOCIAL INSURANCE NO.

L

(Bubbles 0–9)

3 LSAC ACCOUNT NUMBER

(Bubbles 0–9)

4 CENTER NUMBER

(Bubbles 0–9)

5 DATE OF BIRTH

MONTH	DAY	YEAR
○ Jan		
○ Feb		
○ Mar	0 0 0	
○ Apr	1 1 1	1
○ May	2 2 2	
○ June	3 3	
○ July	4 4	4
○ Aug	5 5	5
○ Sept	6 6	6
○ Oct	7 7	7
○ Nov	8 8	8
○ Dec	9 9	9

6 TEST FORM CODE

(Bubbles 0–9)

7 RACIAL/ETHNIC DESCRIPTION
Mark one or more
○ 1 Amer. Indian/Alaska N
○ 2 Asian
○ 3 Black/African Ameri
○ 4 Canadian Aboriginal
○ 5 Caucasian/White
○ 6 Hispanic/Latino
○ 7 Native Hawaiian/ Other Pacific Island
○ 8 Puerto Rican
○ 9 TSI/Aboriginal Austr

8 GENDER
○ Male
○ Female

9 DOMINANT LANGUAGE
○ English
○ Other

10 ENGLISH FLUENCY
○ Yes
○ No

11 TEST DATE

_____ / _____ / _____
MONTH   DAY   YEAR

12 TEST FORM

Law School Admission Test

Mark one and only one answer to each question. Be sure to fill in completely the space for your intended answer choice. If you erase, do so completely. Make no stray marks.

13 TEST BOOK SERIAL NO.

(Bubbles A–T and 0–9)

SECTION 1	SECTION 2	SECTION 3	SECTION 4	SECTION 5
1 A B C D E	1 A B C D E	1 A B C D E	1 A B C D E	1 A B C D E
2 A B C D E	2 A B C D E	2 A B C D E	2 A B C D E	2 A B C D E
3 A B C D E	3 A B C D E	3 A B C D E	3 A B C D E	3 A B C D E
4 A B C D E	4 A B C D E	4 A B C D E	4 A B C D E	4 A B C D E
5 A B C D E	5 A B C D E	5 A B C D E	5 A B C D E	5 A B C D E
6 A B C D E	6 A B C D E	6 A B C D E	6 A B C D E	6 A B C D E
7 A B C D E	7 A B C D E	7 A B C D E	7 A B C D E	7 A B C D E
8 A B C D E	8 A B C D E	8 A B C D E	8 A B C D E	8 A B C D E
9 A B C D E	9 A B C D E	9 A B C D E	9 A B C D E	9 A B C D E
10 A B C D E	10 A B C D E	10 A B C D E	10 A B C D E	10 A B C D E
11 A B C D E	11 A B C D E	11 A B C D E	11 A B C D E	11 A B C D E
12 A B C D E	12 A B C D E	12 A B C D E	12 A B C D E	12 A B C D E
13 A B C D E	13 A B C D E	13 A B C D E	13 A B C D E	13 A B C D E
14 A B C D E	14 A B C D E	14 A B C D E	14 A B C D E	14 A B C D E
15 A B C D E	15 A B C D E	15 A B C D E	15 A B C D E	15 A B C D E
16 A B C D E	16 A B C D E	16 A B C D E	16 A B C D E	16 A B C D E
17 A B C D E	17 A B C D E	17 A B C D E	17 A B C D E	17 A B C D E
18 A B C D E	18 A B C D E	18 A B C D E	18 A B C D E	18 A B C D E
19 A B C D E	19 A B C D E	19 A B C D E	19 A B C D E	19 A B C D E
20 A B C D E	20 A B C D E	20 A B C D E	20 A B C D E	20 A B C D E
21 A B C D E	21 A B C D E	21 A B C D E	21 A B C D E	21 A B C D E
22 A B C D E	22 A B C D E	22 A B C D E	22 A B C D E	22 A B C D E
23 A B C D E	23 A B C D E	23 A B C D E	23 A B C D E	23 A B C D E
24 A B C D E	24 A B C D E	24 A B C D E	24 A B C D E	24 A B C D E
25 A B C D E	25 A B C D E	25 A B C D E	25 A B C D E	25 A B C D E
26 A B C D E	26 A B C D E	26 A B C D E	26 A B C D E	26 A B C D E
27 A B C D E	27 A B C D E	27 A B C D E	27 A B C D E	27 A B C D E
28 A B C D E	28 A B C D E	28 A B C D E	28 A B C D E	28 A B C D E
29 A B C D E	29 A B C D E	29 A B C D E	29 A B C D E	29 A B C D E
30 A B C D E	30 A B C D E	30 A B C D E	30 A B C D E	30 A B C D E

14 PLEASE PRINT INFORMATION

LAST NAME

FIRST NAME

DATE OF BIRTH

THE PREPTEST

- Logical Reasoning ....SECTION I

- Analytical Reasoning.......................................SECTION II

- Reading Comprehension...............................SECTION III

- Logical Reasoning ....SECTION IV

- Writing Sample Materials

Time—35 minutes
25 Questions

Directions: The questions in this section are based on the reasoning contained in brief statements or passages. For some questions, more than one of the choices could conceivably answer the question. However, you are to choose the best answer; that is, the response that most accurately and completely answers the question. You should not make assumptions that are by commonsense standards implausible, superfluous, or incompatible with the passage. After you have chosen the best answer, blacken the corresponding space on your answer sheet.

1. Children should be discouraged from reading Jones's books. Reading them is like eating candy, which provides intense, short-term sensory stimulation but leaves one poorly nourished and dulls one's taste for better fare. In other words, the problem with letting children read Jones's books is that _____.

Which one of the following most logically completes the argument above?

(A) it will lead them to develop a taste for candy and sweets
(B) too many children may become frustrated by their difficulty and stop reading altogether
(C) their doing so interferes with the development of appreciation for more challenging literature
(D) their message may undermine the positive teaching done by parents
(E) children may become so enthralled with books that they will want to spend all their time reading

2. Archaeologist: How did the Parthenon's stonemasons manage to carve columns that all bulged outward in the center in precisely the same way? One hypothesis is suggested by the discovery of a scale drawing of a column etched into the stone of a Greek temple at Didyma. The drawing is a profile view of a column surrounded by a grid, which makes it possible to determine the correct width at every height of the column. The stonemasons who carved the Parthenon's columns may have relied on a drawing like the one at Didyma.

Which one of the following, if true, adds the most support for the archaeologist's hypothesis?

(A) Modern attempts to recreate columns like those at the Parthenon have only been partially successful.
(B) The construction of the temple at Didyma was begun over a century after the Parthenon was constructed.
(C) Scale drawings were commonly used in many types of construction in ancient Greece.
(D) The surviving columns at Didyma are almost twice as tall as the columns at the Parthenon.
(E) The Parthenon's stonemasons had considerable experience carving columns before they started work on the Parthenon.

3. Editorial: The government should not fund any part of its health services with lottery revenue. These health services are essential to our community, but lottery revenue could decline at some time in the future, leaving the government scrambling to make up a budget shortfall.

The argument in the editorial most closely conforms to which one of the following principles?

(A) Governments should spend more of their revenue on essential services than on nonessential services.
(B) Essential government services must be funded from reliable sources of revenue.
(C) No government service should be entirely dependent on lottery revenue for its funding.
(D) Governments should consider all health services to be essential to the community.
(E) At least some lottery revenue must be set aside in case of budget shortfalls in the future.

GO ON TO THE NEXT PAGE.

4. Scientist: Rattlesnakes prey on young California ground squirrels. Protective adult squirrels harass a threatening rattlesnake by puffing up their tails and wagging them. New results show that the squirrel's tail also heats up when harassing a rattlesnake. Since rattlesnakes have an infrared sensing organ that detects body heat, the heating up of the squirrel's tail probably plays a role in repelling rattlesnakes.

Which one of the following, if true, most helps to support the scientist's hypothesis?

(A) Rattlesnakes do not have the ability to increase the temperature of their tails.

(B) Squirrels puff up their tails and wag them when they attempt to attract the attention of other squirrels.

(C) Rattlesnakes react much more defensively when confronted with a squirrel whose tail is heated up than when confronted with one whose tail is not.

(D) The rattlesnake is not the only predator of the California ground squirrel that causes it to engage in harassing behavior as a defensive mechanism.

(E) Mammals such as the California ground squirrel have no organ for sensing infrared energy.

5. Critic: Fillmore, an influential television executive, argues that watching television regularly is not detrimental to very young children. Fillmore bases this on the claim, which I grant, that children can learn much that is beneficial from television. But we should reject Fillmore's argument, because clearly it is to Fillmore's benefit to convince parents that television is not harmful to their children.

Which one of the following most accurately describes a flaw in the critic's reasoning?

(A) It takes a necessary condition for something's being harmful to be a sufficient condition for being harmful.

(B) It concludes that something is true merely on the grounds that there is no evidence to the contrary.

(C) It rejects an argument solely on the grounds that the argument could serve the interests of the person making that argument.

(D) It is based on an appeal to the views of someone with questionable authority on the subject matter.

(E) It bases its conclusion on claims that are inconsistent with one another.

6. While grapefruit juice is a healthy drink, it has been discovered that a chemical in the juice affects how certain medicines are absorbed, with the result that normal medicinal doses act like higher doses. Getting the wrong dose is dangerous. Since it is always desirable to take the lowest effective dose, the best medical approach would be to take lower doses of these medicines along with prescribed amounts of grapefruit juice.

Which one of the following, if true, most seriously weakens the argument?

(A) The amount of the chemical in grapefruit juice is highly unpredictable from glass to glass.

(B) Grapefruit juice is less expensive than most of the medicines with which it interacts.

(C) When scientists removed the chemical from grapefruit juice, the juice no longer affected how certain medicines were absorbed.

(D) The chemical in grapefruit juice works by inhibiting an enzyme in the body that affects how certain medicines are metabolized.

(E) Long before the chemical in grapefruit juice was identified, doctors were advising patients who took certain medicines to avoid grapefruit juice.

7. A landlord needed to replace the air-conditioning unit in a small rental home. The salesperson at the appliance store showed the landlord two air-conditioning units with identical prices. She told the landlord that the Sno-Queen was the most powerful unit for the price, but advised him to purchase the less powerful FreezAll unit, saying that the FreezAll was powerful enough for his needs.

The salesperson's advice to the landlord most closely conforms to which one of the following principles?

(A) When the prices of two different brands of a particular home appliance are identical, either of the products can satisfy the needs of the consumer.

(B) When a consumer is choosing between two different brands of a particular home appliance, the consumer should select the less powerful product only if it is also less expensive.

(C) A salesperson should always recommend that a customer buy the product that represents the best value.

(D) When advising customers about a purchase of a home appliance, a salesperson should direct the customer toward the product that yields the highest commission for the salesperson.

(E) When a consumer is choosing a home appliance, that consumer should choose the least powerful product that meets his or her needs.

8. Editorial: Our political discussions tend to focus largely on the flaws of our nation's leaders, but we need to remind ourselves that these leaders were chosen democratically. The real question that needs answering is how our nation's institutions and procedures enable such people to attain positions of power. Thus, to focus our attention on the flaws of our leaders is to indulge in a pointless distraction.

    Which one of the following is an assumption that the argument requires?

    (A) Examining an individual leader's personal flaws does not reveal anything about how the nation's institutions and procedures influence the selection of leaders.
    (B) Political discussions that focus on the flaws of the nation's leaders will become even more common if the nation's institutions and procedures are not examined.
    (C) The workings of the nation's current institutions and procedures ensure that only flawed individuals will attain positions of power.
    (D) As yet, no one in the nation has made the effort to critically examine the details of the nation's institutions and procedures.
    (E) Concentrating on the flaws of the nation's leaders creates greater dissatisfaction with those leaders.

9. Many calcium supplements contain lead, a potentially dangerous substance even in small amounts. The body can safely store in bones trace amounts of lead from food, but high levels of lead in the blood are a major public health concern, associated with anemia and nerve damage. Despite this, many doctors contend that for some people calcium supplements containing lead are preferable to no calcium supplements at all.

    Which one of the following, if true, would most help to resolve the apparent discrepancy in the information above?

    (A) Some fruits and vegetables contain trace amounts of lead derived from the soil in which they are grown.
    (B) It is difficult to ensure that one has completely eliminated trace amounts of lead from one's diet.
    (C) Lead is only one of the common public health concerns that are associated with anemia and nerve damage.
    (D) A high-calcium diet decreases the amount of lead that the body is able to tolerate safely.
    (E) When calcium intake is insufficient, the body draws calcium from bones, releasing stored lead into the bloodstream.

10. Principle: People should buy an expensive antique only if they can be confident of its authenticity and they find the piece desirable for its intrinsic qualities and not just for its value as an investment.

    Application: Matilde should not buy the expensive antique vase offered for sale on the Internet.

    Which one of the following, if true, most helps to justify the above application of the principle?

    (A) While this style of vase is not currently sought after by other collectors, Matilde has acquired quite a few similar pieces and has developed significant expertise in identifying counterfeits.
    (B) Although the seller is willing to take back the vase if Matilde cannot independently authenticate it, Matilde is not sure that the vase will appreciate much in value in the future.
    (C) The seller of the vase has offered documentation of its age and origin, and Matilde is highly attracted to its shape and color; moreover, she suspects that it will be highly desirable to other collectors in the future.
    (D) The asking price for the vase is significantly less than the amount Matilde thinks it is worth, and the vase is of a style that Matilde particularly likes.
    (E) While Matilde likes the color and features of the vase, its particular style has frequently been reproduced for the mass market, and the vase cannot be examined closely or authenticated over the Internet.

GO ON TO THE NEXT PAGE.

11. Critic: In her presentation of important works of art in
     her art history textbook, Waverly claims to have
     presented only objective accounts: "I have sought
     neither to advocate nor to denigrate what I
     included." In writing about art, a pretense of
     objectivity never succeeds: clearly, Waverly
     writes much better about art she likes than about
     art to which she is indifferent.

The critic's statements, if true, most strongly support
which one of the following?

(A) Waverly believes that a historian of art should
     not prefer certain works of art to other works
     of art.
(B) Waverly has only included works of art that
     she has strong opinions about in her textbook.
(C) Waverly wrote her textbook with the intention of
     advocating the works of art that she likes best.
(D) Waverly has not succeeded in her intended
     objectivity about works of art discussed in
     her textbook.
(E) Waverly does not really believe that objectivity
     is a desirable trait in an art history textbook.

12. Archaeologists are discovering a great deal about the
     Sals culture. For example, recent excavations have
     unearthed smelting furnaces and tools of smelted copper
     and bronze. There were distinct Sals words for copper
     and for bronze, but none for iron. Thus, the Sals did
     not smelt iron.

The conclusion drawn above follows logically if which
one of the following is assumed?

(A) If a culture had a distinct word for a metal,
     then it smelted that metal.
(B) If a culture was unfamiliar with a metal, then it
     did not have a distinct word for that metal.
(C) If a culture smelted copper and bronze, then it
     had distinct words for copper and bronze.
(D) If a culture did not smelt a metal, then it was
     unfamiliar with that metal.
(E) If a culture smelted a metal, then it had a
     distinct word for that metal.

13. Community organizations wanting to enhance support
     for higher education programs need to convince the public
     that such programs benefit society as a whole. Taking
     this approach makes the public more receptive. It is
     much easier, for example, to get the public to support
     road building, which is seen as benefiting everyone,
     than it is to get them to support programs that are seen
     as benefiting only a relatively small segment of society.

Which one of the following most accurately expresses
the overall conclusion drawn in the argument?

(A) Community organizations seeking to encourage
     higher education programs must persuade the
     public that these programs benefit society as
     a whole.
(B) It is easier to get the public to support programs
     that are seen as benefiting everyone than it is
     to get them to support programs that are seen
     as benefiting only a small segment of society.
(C) It is easy to get the public to support road
     building, because road building is seen as
     benefiting society as a whole.
(D) Convincing the public that higher education
     programs will benefit society as a whole makes
     the public more receptive to those programs.
(E) Higher education is similar to road building in
     that both are beneficial to society as a whole.

14. Currently, no satellite orbiting Earth is at significant risk
     of colliding with other satellites or satellite fragments,
     but the risk of such a collision is likely to increase
     dramatically in the future. After all, once such a collision
     occurs, it will probably produce thousands of satellite
     fragments, each large enough to shatter other satellites.
     The resulting collisions will produce many more fragments,
     and so on, causing the space around Earth to become
     quite heavily cluttered with dangerous debris.

Which one of the following most accurately describes
the role played in the argument by the claim that the
risk of a satellite orbiting Earth colliding with other
satellites or satellite fragments is likely to increase
dramatically in the future?

(A) It is an unsupported claim that is used to provide
     support for the argument's conclusion.
(B) It is an unsupported claim that is used to
     support another claim that in turn supports the
     argument's conclusion.
(C) It is a claim for which the argument provides
     some support, and which in turn is used to
     support the argument's conclusion.
(D) It is a claim that serves as the argument's
     conclusion.
(E) It is a claim that provides nonessential background
     information for the argument's conclusion.

GO ON TO THE NEXT PAGE.

15. Researcher: *Salmonella* bacteria are a major cause of illness in humans who consume poultry. Young chicks that underwent a new treatment exhibited a lower incidence of *Salmonella* infection than did untreated chicks, although one week after the treatment was administered the treated chicks had higher concentrations of a variety of bacteria than did untreated chicks.

Which one of the following, if true, most helps to explain the concentrations of bacteria one week after the treatment?

(A) The new treatment takes several weeks to administer.

(B) Levels of *Salmonella* bacteria in young chicks are generally not high to begin with.

(C) Most chicks develop resistance to many harmful bacteria by the time they reach adulthood.

(D) The untreated chicks experienced a higher incidence of illness from infection by bacteria other than *Salmonella* than did treated chicks.

(E) The bacteria found in the treated chicks were nonvirulent types whose growth is inhibited by *Salmonella* bacteria.

16. Debater: As a pedagogical practice, lecturing embodies hierarchy, since the lecturer is superior to the student in mastery of the subject. But people learn best from peer interaction. Thus, the hierarchy in lecturing is a great weakness.

Respondent: By definition, all teaching and learning are hierarchical, for all teaching and learning must proceed from simple to complex. In teaching mathematics, for example, arithmetic must precede calculus. Thus, the hierarchy in lecturing is a strength.

The respondent's reply to the debater's argument is most vulnerable to criticism on the grounds that the respondent

(A) concedes one of the major assumptions on which the debater's argument depends

(B) takes for granted that teaching methods that are effective in mathematics are also effective in other academic disciplines

(C) fails to consider the possibility that some characteristics of lecturing other than hierarchy are weaknesses

(D) applies a key concept to a different aspect of education than the aspect to which the debater applied it

(E) takes for granted that the conceptual structure of mathematics is sufficiently representative of the conceptual structure of at least some other academic disciplines

17. How the pigment known as Han purple was synthesized by the ancient Chinese of the Qin and Han dynasties has puzzled scientists. The Chinese chemists employed the same chemical ingredients used for Han purple in the production of a common type of white glass during that period. Both were produced in processes that involved subjecting the mixtures to high heat and mixing in lead to decrease the melting temperature. Thus, Han purple was probably discovered by fortuitous accident during glass production.

Which one of the following, if true, would most strengthen the argument?

(A) Chemical analysis shows that most of the known fragments of both Han purple and the white glass were produced within a small geographical radius.

(B) Han purple was used for luxury and ceremonial items, whereas the white glass was used to make certain household items.

(C) The technique used for producing Han purple was known to very few people during the Qin and Han dynasties.

(D) The ingredients used in producing both Han purple and the white glass were easily obtainable during the Qin and Han dynasties.

(E) The white glass is found in more surviving artifacts from the Qin and Han dynasties than Han purple is.

GO ON TO THE NEXT PAGE.

18. Medical researcher: A survey of more than 1 million adults found that there was a greater frequency of illness among people who regularly slept at least 8 hours a night than among people who slept significantly less. This shows that mild sleep deprivation is not unhealthy and, in fact, probably bolsters the body's defenses against illness.

The reasoning in the medical researcher's argument is most vulnerable to criticism on the grounds that the argument

(A) fails to address the possibility that an observed correlation between two phenomena is due to another factor that causally contributes to both phenomena

(B) fails to consider that even if a given factor causally contributes to the occurrence of a given phenomenon, it may not be the only factor affecting the occurrence of that phenomenon

(C) concludes, from the claim that a certain phenomenon occurs and the claim that a certain condition is sufficient for that phenomenon to occur, that the condition also exists

(D) takes for granted that there will be an observable correlation between two phenomena if either of those phenomena causally contributes to the other

(E) fails to consider that even if a specific negative consequence is not associated with a given phenomenon, that phenomenon may have other negative consequences

19. If temperatures had dropped below freezing when I was gone last week, the impatiens in my garden would have died. If the impatiens had died, they obviously could not continue to bloom. However, since the impatiens in my garden are still in bloom today, temperatures did not drop below freezing last week.

The pattern of reasoning in which one of the following arguments most closely parallels that in the argument above?

(A) If a species is highly adaptable, it will thrive when introduced into a new environment. If a species thrives in its new environment, it will have an adverse effect on species already existing in that environment. But, since this species has not had an adverse effect on any species already existing in its new environment, it is not highly adaptable.

(B) If a species thrives in a new environment, that species is adaptable. Species that adapt to new environments adversely affect some species already existing in those environments. So, if a species does not adversely affect any species already existing in its new environment, it has not adapted to it.

(C) If a species is introduced into a new environment, it adversely affects some species already existing in that environment, but only if it adapts well to it. Therefore, if a species does not adapt well to a new environment, it will not adversely affect any species already existing in it.

(D) If the introduction of a new species would adversely affect some species already existing in an environment, that species should not be introduced into it. Therefore, since the introduction of species into new environments will result in some species in those environments being adversely affected, species should probably not be introduced into new environments.

(E) If a new species would damage an environment, that species should not be introduced into it. If a new species is introduced, the risk can be reduced by controlling its population. Therefore, because the introduction of species into new environments is likely to happen, their populations should be controlled.

GO ON TO THE NEXT PAGE.

20. If the city builds the proposed convention center, several national professional organizations will hold conventions there. And if several large conventions are held in the city, the total number of visitors will of course increase. Tax revenues will certainly increase if the number of visitors increases. Thus, building the convention center will increase the city's tax revenues.

The conclusion of the argument follows logically if which one of the following is assumed?

(A) If the number of visitors to the city does not increase, then the city's tax revenues will not increase.
(B) If the number of visitors to the city increases, then the amount of money spent by visitors will increase.
(C) The city's tax revenues will not increase unless the convention center is built.
(D) People who are now regular visitors to the city will continue to visit the city if the new convention center is built.
(E) If several national professional organizations hold their conventions in the convention center, those conventions will be large.

21. In a study, pairs of trained dogs were placed side by side and given a command such as "sit." After both obeyed the command, one dog was given a treat while its partner was given no reward at all. Over time, the dogs who went unrewarded began to disobey the command. This shows that dogs have an aversion to being treated unfairly.

Which one of the following would be most useful to know in order to evaluate the argument?

(A) Were dogs who were accustomed to receiving regular rewards prior to the study more inclined to obey the command?
(B) Is there a decline in obedience if rewards are withheld from both dogs in the pair?
(C) Were dogs who received treats in one trial ever used as dogs that did not receive treats in other trials?
(D) Were there any cases in which the dog who was given a reward became more inclined to obey the command?
(E) How many repetitions were required before the unrewarded dogs began to disobey the command?

22. A study of 20,000 20- to 64-year-olds found that people's satisfaction with their incomes is not strongly correlated with the amount they make. People tend to live in neighborhoods of people from their same economic class, and the study shows that people's satisfaction with their incomes depends largely on how favorably their incomes compare with those of their neighbors.

The statements above, if true, most strongly support which one of the following hypotheses?

(A) People with high incomes are consistently more satisfied with their incomes than are people in the middle class.
(B) Older people are generally more satisfied with their incomes than are younger people.
(C) Satisfaction with income is strongly correlated with neighborhood.
(D) In general, people's income levels have little effect on their level of satisfaction with life as a whole.
(E) An increase in everyone's incomes is not likely to greatly increase people's levels of satisfaction with their own incomes.

23. Geologist: The dominant view that petroleum formed from the fossilized remains of plants and animals deep in the earth's crust has been challenged by scientists who hold that it formed, not from living material, but from deep carbon deposits dating from the formation of the earth. But their theory is refuted by the presence in petroleum of biomarkers, molecules indicating the past or present existence of a living organism.

Which one of the following, if true, most weakens the geologist's argument?

(A) Fossils have been discovered that are devoid of biomarkers.
(B) Living organisms only emerged long after the earth's formation.
(C) It would take many millions of years for organisms to become petroleum.
(D) Certain strains of bacteria thrive deep inside the earth's crust.
(E) Some carbon deposits were formed from the fossilized remains of plants.

GO ON TO THE NEXT PAGE.

24. Any driver involved in an accident leading to personal injury or property damage exceeding $500 is legally required to report the accident to the department of motor vehicles, unless the driver is incapable of doing so. Ted is not required to report the accident in which he was involved as a driver.

Which one of the following can be properly inferred from the statements above?

(A) If Ted is incapable of reporting the accident, then the accident did not lead to property damage exceeding $500.

(B) If Ted's car was damaged in excess of $500 in the accident, then he is incapable of reporting the accident to the department of motor vehicles.

(C) Someone other than Ted is legally required to report the accident to the department of motor vehicles.

(D) If Ted is incapable of reporting the accident to the department of motor vehicles, then he was injured in the accident.

(E) Either no one was injured in the accident or the accident did not lead to property damage exceeding $500.

25. Student: If a person has an immunity to infection by a microorganism, then that microorganism does not cause them to develop harmful symptoms. Since many people are exposed to staphylococcus without developing any harmful symptoms, it follows that they have an immunity to infection by this microorganism.

The student's argument is most similar in its flawed pattern of reasoning to which one of the following?

(A) Everything morally right is just, but some actions that best serve the interests of everyone are not just. Thus, some morally right actions do not serve the interests of everyone.

(B) Advertisers try to persuade people that certain claims are true. Since writers of fiction are not advertisers, they probably never try to persuade people that certain claims are true.

(C) Isabel said that she would take the medication. Obviously, though, she did not do so, because medication either cures disease or alleviates its symptoms, and Isabel is still quite ill.

(D) When business owners are subjected to excessive taxation, they become less willing to expand their businesses. The recent decline in business expansions thus shows that their taxes are too high.

(E) Studies show that doctors tend to wash their hands less often than any other health care professionals. This shows that the procedure cannot be of much value in preventing disease.

S T O P

IF YOU FINISH BEFORE TIME IS CALLED, YOU MAY CHECK YOUR WORK ON THIS SECTION ONLY. DO NOT WORK ON ANY OTHER SECTION IN THE TEST.

Time—35 minutes

23 Questions

Directions: Each group of questions in this section is based on a set of conditions. In answering some of the questions, it may be useful to draw a rough diagram. Choose the response that most accurately and completely answers each question and blacken the corresponding space on your answer sheet.

Questions 1–5

A concert is given by a six-member band—guitarist, keyboard player, percussionist, saxophonist, trumpeter, violinist. During the concert, each member performs exactly one solo. The following restrictions apply:

The guitarist does not perform the fourth solo.

The percussionist performs a solo at some time before the keyboard player does.

The keyboard player performs a solo at some time after the violinist does and at some time before the guitarist does.

The saxophonist performs a solo at some time after either the percussionist does or the trumpeter does, but not both.

1. Which one of the following is an acceptable ordering of solos from first to last?

(A) violinist, percussionist, saxophonist, guitarist, trumpeter, keyboard player
(B) percussionist, violinist, keyboard player, trumpeter, saxophonist, guitarist
(C) violinist, trumpeter, saxophonist, percussionist, keyboard player, guitarist
(D) keyboard player, trumpeter, violinist, saxophonist, guitarist, percussionist
(E) guitarist, violinist, keyboard player, percussionist, saxophonist, trumpeter

GO ON TO THE NEXT PAGE.

2. If the percussionist performs a solo at some time before the saxophonist does, then which one of the following must be true?

(A) The percussionist performs the first solo.
(B) The percussionist performs the second solo.
(C) The violinist performs a solo at some time before the saxophonist does.
(D) The percussionist performs a solo at some time before the trumpeter does.
(E) The saxophonist performs a solo at some time before the keyboard player does.

3. Each of the following must be false EXCEPT:

(A) The keyboard player performs the first solo.
(B) The guitarist performs the second solo.
(C) The guitarist performs a solo at some time before the saxophonist does.
(D) The guitarist performs a solo at some time before the percussionist does.
(E) The keyboard player performs a solo at some time before the saxophonist does.

4. Which one of the following CANNOT perform the third solo?

(A) guitarist
(B) keyboard player
(C) saxophonist
(D) trumpeter
(E) violinist

5. If the violinist performs the fourth solo, then each of the following must be true EXCEPT:

(A) The percussionist performs a solo at some time before the violinist does.
(B) The trumpeter performs a solo at some time before the violinist does.
(C) The trumpeter performs a solo at some time before the guitarist does.
(D) The saxophonist performs a solo at some time before the violinist does.
(E) The trumpeter performs a solo at some time before the saxophonist does.

GO ON TO THE NEXT PAGE.

Questions 6–10

Four art historians—Farley, Garcia, Holden, and Jiang—will give a series of four public lectures, each lecture on a different topic—lithographs, oil paintings, sculptures, and watercolors. The lectures will be given one at a time, with each art historian giving a lecture on a different one of the topics. The schedule of the lectures is subject to the following constraints:

The oil paintings lecture and the watercolors lecture must both be earlier than the lithographs lecture.

Farley's lecture must be earlier than the oil paintings lecture.

Holden's lecture must be earlier than both Garcia's lecture and Jiang's lecture.

6. Which one of the following is an acceptable ordering of the lectures, from first to fourth?

(A) Farley: sculptures; Holden: lithographs; Garcia: oil paintings; Jiang: watercolors

(B) Farley: watercolors; Jiang: oil paintings; Holden: sculptures; Garcia: lithographs

(C) Garcia: sculptures; Farley: watercolors; Holden: oil paintings; Jiang: lithographs

(D) Holden: oil paintings; Jiang: watercolors; Farley: lithographs; Garcia: sculptures

(E) Holden: sculptures; Farley: watercolors; Jiang: oil paintings; Garcia: lithographs

GO ON TO THE NEXT PAGE.

7. Which one of the following must be true?

    (A)   Farley's lecture is earlier than the sculptures
            lecture.
    (B)   Holden's lecture is earlier than the lithographs
            lecture.
    (C)   The sculptures lecture is earlier than Garcia's
            lecture.
    (D)   The sculptures lecture is earlier than Jiang's
            lecture.
    (E)   The watercolors lecture is earlier than Garcia's
            lecture.

8. If the watercolors lecture is third, which one of the
   following could be true?

    (A)   Farley gives the watercolors lecture.
    (B)   Garcia gives the oil paintings lecture.
    (C)   Garcia gives the sculptures lecture.
    (D)   Holden gives the sculptures lecture.
    (E)   Jiang gives the lithographs lecture.

9. Which one of the following CANNOT be true?

    (A)   Farley gives the lithographs lecture.
    (B)   Garcia gives the sculptures lecture.
    (C)   Garcia gives the watercolors lecture.
    (D)   Holden gives the oil paintings lecture.
    (E)   Jiang gives the watercolors lecture.

10. If Garcia gives the sculptures lecture, which one of the
    following could be true?

    (A)   The lithographs lecture is third.
    (B)   The oil paintings lecture is third.
    (C)   The sculptures lecture is first.
    (D)   The sculptures lecture is second.
    (E)   The watercolors lecture is second.

GO ON TO THE NEXT PAGE.

<u>Questions 11–16</u>

Three rugs will be woven out of colored thread. Six colors of thread are available—forest, olive, peach, turquoise, white, and yellow—exactly five of which will be used to weave the rugs. Each color that is used will be used in only one of the rugs. The rugs are either solid—woven in a single color—or multicolored. The rugs must be woven according to the following rules:

    In any rug in which white is used, two other colors are also used.
    In any rug in which olive is used, peach is also used.
    Forest and turquoise are not used together in a rug.
    Peach and turquoise are not used together in a rug.
    Peach and yellow are not used together in a rug.

11. Which one of the following could be the colors of the three rugs?

(A)   forest only;
    turquoise only;
    olive, peach, and white

(B)   forest only;
    turquoise only;
    olive, peach, and yellow

(C)   peach only;
    turquoise only;
    forest, olive, and white

(D)   yellow only;
    forest and turquoise;
    olive and peach

(E)   yellow only;
    olive and peach;
    turquoise and white

GO ON TO THE NEXT PAGE.

12. Which one of the following must be true?

   (A)   There are no multicolored rugs in which forest
          is used.
   (B)   There are no multicolored rugs in which
          turquoise is used.
   (C)   Peach is used in one of the rugs.
   (D)   Turquoise is used in one of the rugs.
   (E)   Yellow is used in one of the rugs.

13. If one of the rugs is solid peach, which one of the
    following must be true?

   (A)   One of the rugs is solid forest.
   (B)   One of the rugs is solid turquoise.
   (C)   One of the rugs is solid yellow.
   (D)   Forest and white are used together in a rug.
   (E)   White and yellow are used together in a rug.

14. If there are exactly two solid rugs, then the colors of
    those two rugs CANNOT be

   (A)   forest and peach
   (B)   forest and yellow
   (C)   peach and turquoise
   (D)   peach and yellow
   (E)   turquoise and yellow

15. If forest and peach are used together in a rug, which
    one of the following could be true?

   (A)   There is exactly one solid rug.
   (B)   White is not used in any of the rugs.
   (C)   Yellow is not used in any of the rugs.
   (D)   Turquoise and white are used together in a rug.
   (E)   Turquoise and yellow are used together in a rug.

16. If one of the rugs is solid yellow, then any of the
    following could be true EXCEPT:

   (A)   There is exactly one solid color rug.
   (B)   One of the rugs is solid forest.
   (C)   Turquoise is not used in any of the rugs.
   (D)   Forest and olive are used together in a rug.
   (E)   Peach and white are used together in a rug.

GO ON TO THE NEXT PAGE.

Questions 17–23

The manager of a photography business must assign at least two photographers to each of two graduation ceremonies—one at Silva University and the other at Thorne University. Exactly six photographers are available—Frost, Gonzalez, Heideck, Knutson, Lai, and Mays—but not all have to be assigned. No photographer can be assigned to both ceremonies. The following constraints apply:

  Frost must be assigned together with Heideck to one of the graduation ceremonies.

  If Lai and Mays are both assigned, it must be to different ceremonies.

  If Gonzalez is assigned to the Silva University ceremony, then Lai must be assigned to the Thorne University ceremony.

  If Knutson is not assigned to the Thorne University ceremony, then both Heideck and Mays must be assigned to it.

17. Which one of the following is an acceptable assignment of photographers to the two graduation ceremonies?

(A) Silva University: Gonzalez, Lai
    Thorne University: Frost, Heideck, Mays

(B) Silva University: Gonzalez, Mays
    Thorne University: Knutson, Lai

(C) Silva University: Frost, Gonzalez, Heideck
    Thorne University: Knutson, Lai, Mays

(D) Silva University: Frost, Heideck, Mays
    Thorne University: Gonzalez, Lai

(E) Silva University: Frost, Heideck, Mays
    Thorne University: Gonzalez, Knutson, Lai

GO ON TO THE NEXT PAGE.

18. If Heideck is assigned to the same graduation ceremony as Lai, then which one of the following must be true?

    (A) Frost is assigned to the Thorne University ceremony.
    (B) Gonzalez is assigned to the Silva University ceremony.
    (C) Gonzalez is assigned to neither graduation ceremony.
    (D) Knutson is assigned to the Thorne University ceremony.
    (E) Lai is assigned to the Thorne University ceremony.

19. Which one of the following could be the complete assignment of photographers to the Silva University ceremony?

    (A) Frost, Gonzalez, Heideck, Knutson
    (B) Frost, Gonzalez, Heideck
    (C) Gonzalez, Knutson
    (D) Heideck, Lai
    (E) Knutson, Mays

20. Which one of the following is a complete and accurate list of all of the photographers who must be assigned?

    (A) Frost, Heideck
    (B) Frost, Heideck, Knutson
    (C) Frost, Heideck, Knutson, Lai
    (D) Frost, Gonzalez, Heideck
    (E) Frost, Gonzalez, Heideck, Mays

21. If exactly four of the photographers are assigned to the graduation ceremonies, then which one of the following must be assigned to the Silva University ceremony?

    (A) Frost
    (B) Gonzalez
    (C) Knutson
    (D) Lai
    (E) Mays

22. Which one of the following CANNOT be the complete assignment of photographers to the Thorne University ceremony?

    (A) Frost, Gonzalez, Heideck, Mays
    (B) Frost, Heideck, Knutson, Mays
    (C) Gonzalez, Knutson, Lai
    (D) Gonzalez, Knutson, Mays
    (E) Knutson, Mays

23. Which one of the following, if substituted for the constraint that if Knutson is not assigned to the Thorne University ceremony, then both Heideck and Mays must be assigned to it, would have the same effect in determining the assignment of photographers to the graduation ceremonies?

    (A) If Knutson is assigned to the Silva University ceremony, then Heideck and Mays cannot both be assigned to that ceremony.
    (B) If Knutson is assigned to the Silva University ceremony, then Lai must also be assigned to that ceremony.
    (C) Unless Knutson is assigned to the Thorne University ceremony, both Frost and Mays must be assigned to that ceremony.
    (D) Unless Knutson is assigned to the Thorne University ceremony, Heideck cannot be assigned to the same ceremony as Lai.
    (E) Unless either Heideck or Mays is assigned to the Thorne University ceremony, Knutson must be assigned to that ceremony.

S T O P

IF YOU FINISH BEFORE TIME IS CALLED, YOU MAY CHECK YOUR WORK ON THIS SECTION ONLY.
DO NOT WORK ON ANY OTHER SECTION IN THE TEST.

Time—35 minutes
27 Questions

<u>Directions</u>: Each set of questions in this section is based on a single passage or a pair of passages. The questions are to be answered on the basis of what is <u>stated</u> or <u>implied</u> in the passage or pair of passages. For some of the questions, more than one of the choices could conceivably answer the question. However, you are to choose the <u>best</u> answer; that is, the response that most accurately and completely answers the question, and blacken the corresponding space on your answer sheet.

Given the amount of time and effort that curators, collectors, dealers, scholars, and critics spend on formulating judgments of taste in relation to oil paintings, it seems odd that so few are prepared to
(5) apply some of the same skills in exploring works of art that stimulate another sense altogether: that of smell. Why is great perfume not taken more seriously? While art professionals are very serious about many branches of literature, architecture, and music, I have
(10) yet to find a curatorial colleague who regularly beats a path to the fragrance counter in search of, say, *Joy Parfum*, the 1930 masterpiece by Henri Alméras.

And yet, the parallels between what ought to be regarded as sister arts are undeniable. Painters
(15) combine natural and, these days, synthetic pigments with media such as oils and resins, much as the perfumer carefully formulates natural and synthetic chemical compounds. The Old Masters deployed oil paint across the color spectrum, and applied layers on
(20) a determining ground and various kinds of underpainting, slowly building up to the surface, completing their work with thin glazes on top. Thus various types of mashed-up earth and vegetable suspended in linseed or poppy oil are brushed over a
(25) stretch of woven fabric. They begin to dry, and a picture is born. Its appearance changes over time, because the tendency of oil paint is to become gradually more transparent.

So, too, talented "noses" experiment with
(30) complex configurations of olfactory elements and produce in symphonic combination many small sensations, at times discordant, sweet, bitter, melancholy, or happy, as the case may be. These combinations change and develop in sequence or in
(35) unison as the substance and its constituents evaporate at different rates, some quickly, others slowly, thanks to the warmth of our skin. A brilliant perfumer may thus devise an imaginary world no less powerful, or intimate, than that of a great composer or painter, and
(40) in calling on our capacity to discover there some memory of childhood or of a long-forgotten experience, perfumers are in the same business as the artist who creates the illusion of life on canvas.

Perhaps one reason that truly great smells are so
(45) often undervalued is that perfumes are today made and distributed under the not particularly watchful gaze of a few large corporations. The cynical bean counters in Paris and Zurich do not hesitate to tamper with old formulas, insisting on the substitution of cheap
(50) chemical compounds that approximately resemble rarer, better ingredients in an effort to increase profits.

They do not tell their customers when or how they do this; indeed, they presume their customers won't notice the difference. Consequently, fine perfume is
(55) now hopelessly entangled with the international cosmetic dollar, and ill-served by marketing and public relations.

1. Which one of the following most accurately expresses the main point of the passage?

(A) Despite their pursuit of profit, corporations that produce and market perfumes value artistic skill.

(B) A masterpiece perfume evokes reactions that are no less powerful than those evoked by a masterpiece in music or painting.

(C) The corporate nature of the perfume business is the reason that so few truly great perfumes are now produced.

(D) Great perfumes are works of art and deserve respect and attention as such.

(E) Perfume-making and oil painting should be regarded as sister arts, both of which involve the skilled application of complex configurations of ingredients.

2. In which one of the following circumstances would the author of the passage be most likely to believe that a perfume manufacturer is justified in altering the formula of a classic perfume?

(A) The alteration makes the perfume more closely resemble *Joy Parfum*.

(B) The alteration is done to replace an ingredient that is currently very costly.

(C) The alteration replaces a synthetic chemical compound with a natural chemical compound.

(D) The alteration is done to make the perfume popular with a wider variety of customers.

(E) The alteration takes a previously altered perfume closer to its creator's original formula.

GO ON TO THE NEXT PAGE.

3. The word "noses" (line 29) refers to

   (A) perfumers
   (B) perfume collectors
   (C) particular perfumes
   (D) people with expertise in marketing perfumes
   (E) people with expertise in pricing perfumes

4. The passage provides the most support for which one of the following statements about art?

   (A) A work of art can bring about an aesthetic experience through the memories that it evokes.
   (B) In any work of art, one can detect the harmonious combination of many small sensations.
   (C) A work of art will inevitably fail if it is created for the sake of commercial success.
   (D) The best works of art improve with age.
   (E) Some forms of art are superior to others.

5. The author would be most likely to hold which one of the following opinions about *Joy Parfum* by Henri Alméras?

   (A) As time goes on, its artistry is appreciated more and more.
   (B) As a work of art, it is no less important than a great piece of sculpture.
   (C) It was the foremost accomplishment of its time in perfume making.
   (D) It is a fragrance that is appreciated only by people with refined taste.
   (E) Its original formula is similar to many other perfumes of the 1930s.

6. Which one of the following is most analogous to what the author calls the "cynical bean counters" (line 47)?

   (A) an art museum curator who caters to popular tastes in choosing works for an exhibition
   (B) a movie studio executive who imposes cost-saving production restrictions on a film's director
   (C) a director of an art institute who cuts the annual budget because of projections of declining revenues
   (D) a business executive who convinces her company to invest in art merely for the sake of tax benefits
   (E) an art school dean who slashes the budget of one project in order to increase the budget of his pet project

7. The last paragraph most strongly supports which one of the following statements?

   (A) The names of the world's best perfumes are not known to most customers.
   (B) The profitability of a particular perfume is not a good indicator of its quality.
   (C) Companies that sell perfume pay little attention to what their customers want.
   (D) Perfume makers of the past would never tamper with established formulas.
   (E) Companies that sell perfume make most of their profits on perfumes in the least expensive price ranges.

8. Which one of the following most accurately describes the organization of the passage?

   (A) The first paragraph makes an observation, the middle paragraphs elaborate on that observation while considering one possible explanation for it, and the final paragraph delivers an alternative explanation.
   (B) The first paragraph advances a thesis, the middle paragraphs present a case for that thesis, and the final paragraph considers and rejects one particular challenge to that thesis.
   (C) The first paragraph sets out a challenge to received wisdom, the middle paragraphs present a response to that challenge, and the final paragraph presents a concrete example that supports the response.
   (D) The first paragraph poses a question, the middle paragraphs present a case that helps to justify the posing of that question, and the final paragraph presents a possible answer to the question.
   (E) The first paragraph outlines a problem, the middle paragraphs present two consequences of that problem, and the final paragraph attempts to identify the parties that are responsible for the problem.

GO ON TO THE NEXT PAGE.

"Stealing thunder" is a courtroom strategy that consists in a lawyer's revealing negative information about a client before that information is revealed or elicited by an opposing lawyer. While there is no point
(5) in revealing a weakness that is unknown to one's opponents or that would not be exploited by them, many lawyers believe that if the weakness is likely to be revealed in opposing testimony, it should be volunteered; otherwise, the hostile revelation would
(10) be more damaging.

Although no empirical research has directly tested the effectiveness of stealing thunder in actual trials, studies involving simulated trial situations have suggested that the technique is, in fact, effective, at
(15) least within a reasonably broad range of applications. Lawyers' commonly held belief in the value of stealing thunder is not only corroborated by those experimental findings; it is also supported by several psychological explanations of why the technique
(20) should work. For one thing, volunteering damaging information early may create an image of credibility. Psychological research suggests that people who reveal information that appears to be against their own best interest are likely to be perceived as more credible
(25) and thus may be more persuasive. Stealing thunder may also provide juries with an impetus for critical assessment by previewing, and thus alerting them to, testimony that the opposition plans to present. In psychological experiments, audiences that were
(30) previously warned of an upcoming attempt at persuasion became more resistant to the persuasive attempt, forming counterarguments based on the warning. Also, the value placed on a persuasive message is probably much like the value placed on any
(35) commodity; the scarcer the commodity, the more valuable it is. A persuasive message will thus increase in value and effectiveness to the extent that it is seen as scarce. In the courtroom, a piece of evidence brought by both the prosecution and the defense, as
(40) when thunder is stolen, may be seen as less scarce—becoming "old news." Thus, unless that evidence is of overriding consequence, it should carry less weight than if it had been included only in hostile testimony.

Finally, stealing thunder may work because the
(45) lawyer can frame the evidence in his or her own terms and downplay its significance, just as politicians sometimes seek to put their "spin" on potentially damaging information. However, it may therefore be effective only when the negative information can be
(50) framed positively. Jurors, who often initially have little information about a case, are usually eager to solidify their position regarding the case. They can therefore be expected to use the early positive framing to guide their subsequent analysis of the trial information. But
(55) this also suggests limitations on the use of the technique: when information is very damaging, stealing thunder may create an early negative impression that forms a cognitive framework for jurors, who then filter subsequent information through this schema.

9. Which one of the following most accurately expresses the main point of the passage?

(A) Although there are limits to the usefulness of stealing thunder, its effectiveness in actual trials has been demonstrated through research conducted by psychologists and legal scholars.

(B) The commonly practiced courtroom strategy of stealing thunder can have unintended consequences if the lawyers using it do not accurately predict jurors' attitudes.

(C) Lawyers' commonly held belief in the value of stealing thunder is supported by several psychological explanations of how that strategy may influence jurors.

(D) The risks involved in stealing thunder can outweigh the probable benefits when the information to be revealed is too readily available or too negative in its impact.

(E) Research designed to confirm the usefulness of stealing thunder has vindicated lawyers' belief in the value of the technique and has identified the general limitations of the strategy's effectiveness.

10. It can be most reasonably inferred from the passage that which one of the following is an example of stealing thunder?

(A) warning jurors that a client on the opposing side has a serious conflict of interest and cannot be trusted

(B) disclosing in opening statements of a defense against copyright infringement that one's client has in the past been guilty of plagiarism

(C) responding to the opposition's revelation that one's client has a minor criminal background by conceding that this is the case

(D) pointing out to jurors during opening statements the mistaken reasoning in the opposition's case

(E) stressing that one's client, while technically guilty, is believable and that mitigating circumstances should be considered

11. Which one of the following does the author mention as a factor that in some instances probably contributes to the success of stealing thunder?

(A) careful timing of the thunder-stealing message to precede the opposition's similar message by only a short time

(B) some lawyers' superior skill in assessing jurors' probable reactions to a message

(C) the willingness of some lawyers' clients to testify in person about their own past mistakes

(D) jurors' desire to arrive at a firm view regarding the case they are hearing

(E) lawyers' careful screening of prospective jurors prior to the beginning of courtroom proceedings

GO ON TO THE NEXT PAGE.

12. The author discusses the "cognitive framework" that jurors create (line 58) primarily to

(A) indicate that at least some information mentioned early in a trial can influence the way jurors evaluate information presented later in the trial

(B) indicate that jurors bring into court with them certain attitudes and biases that at least in part inform their opinions during trials

(C) suggest that damaging evidence that is framed positively early in a trial will have a greater impact than damaging evidence presented later in a trial

(D) theorize that stealing thunder is best done as early as possible in a case, before the opposition has an opportunity to solidify jurors' opinions

(E) speculate that creating credibility in some cases is probably more effective than positively framing very harmful information

13. The author's attitude regarding stealing thunder can most accurately be described as

(A) concerned that the technique may become so common that lawyers will fail to recognize its drawbacks

(B) favorable toward its use by lawyers during the opening statements of a case but skeptical of its value otherwise

(C) concerned that research results supporting it may omit crucial anecdotal evidence indicating pitfalls in its use

(D) approving of its use on the grounds that its success is experimentally supported and can be psychologically explained

(E) skeptical of its suitability for use by lawyers without lengthy experience in courtroom strategies

14. The author's characterization of stealing thunder in the passage is based at least partly on both

(A) informal surveys of lawyers' clients' reactions to stealing thunder and controlled research based on simulated trial situations

(B) statistical surveys of lawyers who steal thunder and observations of lawyers' tactics in trials

(C) records of judges' decisions in court cases and the results of studies involving simulated courtroom situations

(D) informal observations of nontrial uses of techniques analogous to stealing thunder and controlled studies of lawyers' courtroom behavior

(E) research that was not directly concerned with legal proceedings and research in which subjects participated in simulated trial situations

15. By saying that certain studies have suggested that in some applications, "the technique is, in fact, effective" (line 14), the author most likely means that those studies have given evidence that the technique in question

(A) inclines juries to regard the clients of those using the technique more favorably than would be the case if the negative information about them were first divulged by the opposition

(B) is a reliable means, in courtroom settings, of introducing a set of counterarguments that jurors will be able to use in resisting the opposition's subsequent attempts at persuasion

(C) invariably results in cases being decided in favor of the clients of those using the technique rather than in favor of parties opposing those clients, if it is used broadly

(D) appears generally to succeed as a means of forcefully capturing jurors' attention and thus leading them to focus more attentively than they would otherwise on the lawyer's message

(E) more often than not achieves its goal of timing a negative revelation so as to dramatically precede the opposition's revelation of the same information

16. The passage most strongly implies that many lawyers believe which one of the following concerning decisions about whether to steal thunder?

(A) A lawyer should be concerned with how readily the negative information can be positively framed, especially if the information is very negative.

(B) A lawyer should take into account, among other things, whether or not the jurors are already familiar with some of the relevant facts of the case prior to the trial.

(C) The decision should be based on careful deliberations that anticipate both positive and negative reactions of jurors and opposing lawyers.

(D) The decision should depend on how probable it is that the opposition will try to derive an advantage from mentioning the negative information in question.

(E) The decision should be based at least partly on a lawyer's knowledge of relevant psychological research findings and legal statistics.

GO ON TO THE NEXT PAGE.

Passage A

To a neuroscientist, you are your brain; nothing causes your behavior other than the operations of your brain. This viewpoint, together with recent findings in neuroscience, radically changes the way we think
(5) about the law. The official line in the law is that all that matters is whether you are rational, but you can have someone who is totally rational even though their strings are being pulled by something beyond their control. Indeed, people who believe themselves to be
(10) making a free and rational moral choice may really be deluding themselves—a brain scan might show that such a choice correlates with activity in emotional centers in the brain rather than in the region of the brain associated with deliberative problem solving.
(15) This insight suggests that the criminal-justice system should abandon the idea of retribution—the idea that bad people should be punished because of their freely chosen immoral acts—which is now dominant as a justification of punishment. Instead, the law should
(20) focus on deterring future harms. In some cases, this might mean lighter punishments. If it is really true that we do not get any prevention bang from our punishment buck when we punish some person, then it is not worth punishing that person.

Passage B

(25) Neuroscience constantly produces new mechanistic descriptions of how the physical brain causes behavior, adding fuel to the deterministic view that all human action is causally necessitated by events that are independent of the will. It has long been
(30) argued, however, that the concept of free will can coexist with determinism.

In 1954 English philosopher Alfred J. Ayer put forth a theory of "soft determinism." He argued, as the philosopher David Hume had two centuries earlier,
(35) that even in a deterministic world, a person can still act freely. Ayer distinguished between free actions and constrained actions. Free actions are those that are caused by internal sources, by one's own will (unless one is suffering from a disorder). Constrained actions
(40) are those that are caused by external sources, for example, by someone or something forcing you physically or mentally to perform an action, as in hypnosis or in mental disorders such as kleptomania. When someone performs a free action to do A, he or
(45) she could have done B instead, since no external source precluded doing so. When someone performs a constrained action to do A, he or she could have done only A.

Ayer argued that actions are free as long as they
(50) are not constrained. It is not the existence of a cause but the source of the cause that determines whether an action is free. Although Ayer did not explicitly discuss the brain's role, one could make the analogy that those actions—and indeed those wills—that originate from
(55) a disease-free brain are not constrained, and are therefore free, even though they may be determined.

17. Both passages are concerned with answering which one of the following questions?

(A) Should people be punished for actions that are outside of their control?
(B) Does scientific research into the brain have implications regarding freedom of the will?
(C) Can actions that are not free be effectively deterred by the threat of punishment?
(D) Is the view that retribution is a legitimate justification for punishment compatible with the findings of neuroscience?
(E) Can an action be free if someone else physically forced the actor to perform it?

18. Which one of the following concepts plays a role in the argument of passage B but not in that of passage A?

(A) mental disorder
(B) free choice
(C) causality
(D) self-delusion
(E) moral responsibility

19. One purpose of the reference by the author of passage B to David Hume (line 34) is to

(A) characterize Ayer as someone who is not an original thinker
(B) add credence to the theory of soft determinism
(C) suggest that the theory of soft determinism is primarily of historical importance
(D) suggest that the theory of soft determinism has been in existence as long as mechanistic descriptions of the brain have
(E) add intellectual respectability to the view that the brain should not be described mechanistically

GO ON TO THE NEXT PAGE.

3

20. Passage B differs from passage A in that passage B displays an attitude toward the ideas it discusses that is more

    (A) engaged
    (B) dismissive
    (C) detached
    (D) ironic
    (E) skeptical

21. Which one of the following arguments is most analogous to the argument advanced in passage A?

    (A) Many word processors are packed with nonessential features that only confuse most users and get in the way of important functions. Word processors with fewer features thus enhance productivity.

    (B) Economic models generally presume that actors in an economy are entirely rational. But psychological studies have documented many ways in which people make irrational choices. Thus, economic models, in theory, should not be able to predict human behavior.

    (C) The existing program for teaching mathematics in elementary schools is based on mistaken notions about what sorts of mathematical concepts children can grasp, and it should therefore be replaced.

    (D) Civil disobedience is justified only in those cases in which civil law conflicts with one's sincere moral or religious convictions. Any attempt to justify civil disobedience on something other than moral or religious grounds is therefore illegitimate.

    (E) Being autonomous does not imply having full control over one's behavior. After all, addicted smokers are unable to exercise control over some behaviors but are nevertheless autonomous in the general sense.

GO ON TO THE NEXT PAGE.

This passage is adapted from a review of a 1991 book.

In a recent study, Mario García argues that in the United States between 1930 and 1960 the group of political activists he calls the "Mexican American Generation" was more radical and politically diverse
(5) than earlier historians have recognized. Through analysis of the work of some of the era's most important scholars, García does provide persuasive evidence that in the 1930s and 1940s these activists anticipated many of the reforms proposed by the more
(10) militant Chicanos of the 1960s and 1970s. His study, however, suffers from two flaws.

First, García's analysis of the evidence he provides to demonstrate the Mexican American Generation's political diversity is not entirely
(15) consistent. Indeed, he undermines his primary thesis by emphasizing an underlying consensus among various groups that tends to conceal the full significance of their differences. Groups such as the League of United Latin American Citizens, an
(20) organization that encouraged Mexican Americans to pursue a civil rights strategy of assimilation into the United States political and cultural mainstream, were often diametrically opposed to organizations such as the Congress of Spanish-Speaking People, a coalition
(25) group that advocated bilingual education and equal rights for resident aliens in the United States. García acknowledges these differences but dismisses them as insignificant, given that the goals of groups as disparate as these centered on liberal reform, not
(30) revolution. But one need only note the fierce controversies that occurred during the period over United States immigration policies and the question of assimilation versus cultural maintenance to recognize that Mexican American political history since 1930
(35) has been characterized not by consensus but by intense and lively debate.

Second, García may be exaggerating the degree to which the views of these activists were representative of the ethnic Mexican population residing in the
(40) United States during this period. Noting that by 1930 the proportion of the Mexican American population that had been born in the United States had significantly increased, García argues that between 1930 and 1960 a new generation of Mexican American
(45) leaders appeared, one that was more acculturated and hence more politically active than its predecessor. Influenced by their experience of discrimination and by the inclusive rhetoric of World War II slogans, these leaders, according to García, were determined to
(50) achieve full civil rights for all United States residents of Mexican descent. However, it is not clear how far this outlook extended beyond these activists. Without a better understanding of the political implications of important variables such as patterns of bilingualism
(55) and rates of Mexican immigration and naturalization, and the variations in ethnic consciousness these variables help to create, one cannot assume that an increase in the proportion of Mexican Americans born in the United States necessarily resulted in an increase
(60) in the ethnic Mexican population's political activism.

22. According to the passage, the League of United Latin American Citizens differed from the Congress of Spanish-Speaking People in that the League of United Latin American Citizens

(A) sought the political goals most popular with other United States citizens
(B) fought for equal rights for resident aliens in the United States
(C) favored a more liberal United States immigration policy
(D) encouraged Mexican Americans to speak Spanish rather than English
(E) encouraged Mexican Americans to adopt the culture of the United States

23. It can be inferred from the passage that García would most probably agree with which one of the following statements about the Mexican American political activists of the 1930s and 1940s?

(A) Some of their concerns were similar to those of the Mexican American activists of the 1960s and 1970s.
(B) They were more politically diverse than the Mexican American activists of the 1960s and 1970s.
(C) They were as militant as the Mexican American activists of the 1960s and 1970s.
(D) Most of them advocated bilingual education and equal rights for resident aliens in the United States.
(E) Most of them were more interested in revolution than in liberal reform.

GO ON TO THE NEXT PAGE.

24. The passage suggests that García assumes which one of the following to have been true of Mexican Americans between 1930 and 1960?

    (A) Increased ethnic consciousness among Mexican Americans accounted for an increase in political activity among them.
    (B) Increased familiarity among Mexican Americans with United States culture accounted for an increase in political activity among them.
    (C) The assimilation of many Mexican Americans into United States culture accounted for Mexican Americans' lack of interest in political activity.
    (D) Many Mexican Americans were moved to political militancy as a means of achieving full civil rights for all United States residents of Mexican descent.
    (E) Many Mexican Americans were moved to political protest by their experience of discrimination and the patronizing rhetoric of World War II slogans.

25. It can be inferred that the author of the passage believes which one of the following about the Mexican American political activists of the 1930s and 1940s?

    (A) Their common goal of liberal reform made them less militant than the Mexican American activists of the 1960s and 1970s.
    (B) Their common goal of liberal reform did not outweigh their political differences.
    (C) Their common goal of liberal reform helped them reach a consensus in spite of their political differences.
    (D) They were more or less evenly divided between those favoring assimilation and those favoring cultural maintenance.
    (E) They did not succeed in fully achieving their political goals because of their disparate political views.

26. The author of the passage expresses uncertainty with regard to which one of the following?

    (A) whether or not one can assume that the increase in the number of Mexican Americans born in the United States led to an increase in Mexican American political activism
    (B) whether or not historians preceding García were correct in their assumptions about Mexican Americans who were politically active between 1930 and 1960
    (C) whether or not there was general consensus among Mexican American political activists between 1930 and 1960
    (D) the extent to which the views of Mexican American activists were shared by the ethnic Mexican population in the United States
    (E) the nature of the relationship between the League of United Latin American Citizens and the Congress of Spanish-Speaking People

27. The passage supports which one of the following statements about ethnic consciousness among Mexican Americans?

    (A) Ethnic consciousness increases when rates of Mexican immigration and naturalization increase.
    (B) Ethnic consciousness increases when the number of Mexican Americans born in the United States increases.
    (C) Ethnic consciousness decreases when the number of Mexican Americans assimilating into the culture of the United States increases.
    (D) Variations in the influence of Mexican American leaders over the Mexican American population at large account in part for variations in ethnic consciousness.
    (E) Variations in rates of Mexican immigration and naturalization account in part for variations in ethnic consciousness.

S T O P

IF YOU FINISH BEFORE TIME IS CALLED, YOU MAY CHECK YOUR WORK ON THIS SECTION ONLY.
DO NOT WORK ON ANY OTHER SECTION IN THE TEST.

Time—35 minutes
26 Questions

Directions: The questions in this section are based on the reasoning contained in brief statements or passages. For some questions, more than one of the choices could conceivably answer the question. However, you are to choose the best answer; that is, the response that most accurately and completely answers the question. You should not make assumptions that are by commonsense standards implausible, superfluous, or incompatible with the passage. After you have chosen the best answer, blacken the corresponding space on your answer sheet.

1.   Ming: Since trans fat is particularly unhealthy, it's
        fortunate for the consumer that so many cookie
        manufacturers have completely eliminated it
        from their products.

     Carol: Why do you say that? Even without trans fat,
        desserts do not make for healthy eating.

     Carol's response indicates that she interpreted Ming's
     remarks to mean that

     (A)   the more trans fat a cookie contains, the more
            unhealthy it is
     (B)   food that doesn't contain trans fat is healthy food
     (C)   if a food is not healthy, then it is unhealthy
     (D)   a cookie containing any amount of trans fat
            is unhealthy
     (E)   consumers should purchase cookies only if they
            do not contain trans fat

2.   Historian: During the Industrial Revolution, for the first
        time in history, the productivity of the economy
        grew at a faster rate than the population and thus
        dramatically improved living standards. An
        economist theorizes that this growth was made
        possible by the spread of values such as hard
        work and thrift. But successful explanations need
        to be based on facts, so no one should accept this
        explanation until historical evidence demonstrates
        that a change in values occurred prior to the
        Industrial Revolution.

     The overall conclusion of the historian's argument is that

     (A)   during the Industrial Revolution the productivity
            of the economy grew at a faster rate than the
            population
     (B)   the fact that the productivity of the economy
            grew at a faster rate than the population during
            the Industrial Revolution led to a dramatic
            improvement in living standards
     (C)   no one should accept the economist's
            explanation until historical evidence
            demonstrates that a change in values occurred
            prior to the Industrial Revolution
     (D)   the improvement in living standards that
            occurred during the Industrial Revolution was
            not due to the spread of a change in values
     (E)   values such as hard work and thrift did not
            become widespread prior to the Industrial
            Revolution

3.   The master plan for the new park calls for the planting
     of trees of any species native to this area, except for
     those native trees that grow to be very large, such as
     the cottonwood. The trees that the community group
     donated were purchased at Three Rivers Nursery, which
     sells mostly native trees and shrubs. Thus, the donated
     trees are probably consistent with the master plan.

     Which one of the following, if true, most strengthens
     the argument?

     (A)   Some tree species that grow to be very large
            are consistent with the master plan.
     (B)   Three Rivers Nursery sells cottonwood trees.
     (C)   Many of the native species that Three Rivers
            Nursery sells are shrubs, not trees.
     (D)   Tree species that are not native to this area and
            that are consistent with the master plan are
            rare and hard to find.
     (E)   Three Rivers Nursery does not sell any tree
            species that grow to be very large.

GO ON TO THE NEXT PAGE.

4. Paleontologists had long supposed that the dinosaur *Diplodocus* browsed for high-growing vegetation such as treetop leaves by raising its very long neck. But now computer models have shown that the structure of *Diplodocus*'s neck bones would have prevented such movement. The neck could, however, bend downward and even extend below ground level, allowing *Diplodocus* to access underwater vegetation from dry land. Thus, *Diplodocus* must have fed on plants on or near the ground, or underwater.

Which one of the following is an assumption required by the argument?

(A) The same type of neck structure is found in modern ground-feeding animals.

(B) *Diplodocus* was not able to see in front of itself unless its head was angled steeply downward.

(C) It would be impossible for a large animal such as *Diplodocus* to supply blood to an elevated brain.

(D) *Diplodocus* had no other way of accessing high-growing vegetation, such as by rising up on its hind legs.

(E) *Diplodocus* was not able to browse for underwater vegetation by kneeling beside bodies of water or by walking into them.

5. Government official: Although the determination of local residents to rebuild hiking trails recently devastated by a landslide indicates that they are strongly committed to their community, the government should not assist them in rebuilding. The reason is clear: there is a strong likelihood of future landslides in that location that could cause serious injury or worse.

Which one of the following principles, if valid, most helps to justify the reasoning in the government official's argument?

(A) Residents should not be allowed to rebuild trails unless the government assists them in rebuilding.

(B) The determination of residents to rebuild hiking trails devastated by landslides should be what determines government support for the project.

(C) Government agencies should not assist people with projects unless those people are strongly committed to their community.

(D) The government should not assist in projects that are very likely to result in circumstances that could lead to serious injury.

(E) Residents should be discouraged from rebuilding in any area that has had an extensive history of landslides.

6. Scientist: There is a lot of concern that human behavior may be responsible for large-scale climate change. But this should be seen as more of an opportunity than a problem. If human behavior is responsible for climate change, then we can control future climate change to make it less extreme than previous climate shifts.

The scientist's argument requires assuming which one of the following?

(A) The same degree of climate change produces less damage if it is caused by human behavior than if it has a purely natural cause.

(B) Human beings can control the aspects of their behavior that have an impact on climate change.

(C) At least some previous large-scale climate changes have been caused by human behavior.

(D) Large-scale climate change poses a greater danger to human beings than to other species.

(E) It is easier to identify the human behaviors that cause climate change than it is to change those behaviors.

7. In a study of heart patients awaiting treatment for reduced blood flow to the heart, those still waiting to find out whether they would need surgery were less likely to experience pain from the condition than were those who knew what type of treatment they would receive. Assuming that this uncertainty is more stressful than knowing what one's future holds, then it is reasonable to conclude that _____.

Which one of the following most logically completes the argument?

(A) stress sometimes reduces the amount of pain a heart patient experiences

(B) the pain experienced by heart patients is to some extent beneficial

(C) the severity of a heart patient's condition is usually worsened by withholding information from the patient about the treatment that that patient will receive

(D) stress is probably an effect rather than a cause of reduced blood flow to the heart

(E) heart patients suffering from reduced blood flow to the heart who are experiencing pain from the condition are more likely to require surgery than are such patients who are not experiencing pain

GO ON TO THE NEXT PAGE.

8. Given the shape of the hip and foot bones of the Kodiak bear, it has been determined that standing and walking upright is completely natural behavior for these bears. Thus, walking on hind legs is instinctive and not a learned behavior of the Kodiak.

To which one of the following criticisms is the argument most vulnerable?

(A) The argument incorrectly generalizes from the behavior of a few bears in support of its conclusion.
(B) The argument fails to consider the possibility that walking on hind legs is the result of both learning and an innate capacity.
(C) The word "behavior" illicitly changes meaning during the course of the argument.
(D) The argument presumes, without giving justification, that all behavior can be explained in one or both of only two ways.
(E) The argument incorrectly appeals to the authority of science in order to support its conclusion.

9. People are usually interested in, and often even moved by, anecdotes about individuals, whereas they rarely even pay attention to statistical information, much less change their beliefs in response to it. However, although anecdotes are generally misleading in that they are about unrepresentative cases, people tend to have fairly accurate beliefs about society.

Which one of the following, if true, would most help to explain why people tend to have accurate beliefs about society despite the facts described above?

(A) Statistical information tends to obscure the characteristics of individuals.
(B) Most people recognize that anecdotes tend to be about unrepresentative cases.
(C) The more emotionally compelling an anecdote is, the more likely it is to change a person's beliefs.
(D) Statistical information is made more comprehensible when illustrated by anecdotes.
(E) People tend to base their beliefs about other people on their emotional response to those people.

10. In 2005, paleontologist Mary Schweitzer made headlines when she reported finding preserved soft tissue in the bones of a *Tyrannosaurus rex* dinosaur. Analysis of the collagen proteins from the *T. rex* showed them to be similar to the collagen proteins in modern-day chickens. Schweitzer's discovery therefore adds to the mountain of evidence that dinosaurs are closely related to birds.

The answer to which one of the following questions would be most useful to know in order to evaluate the argument?

(A) How rare is it to find preserved soft tissue in the bones of a dinosaur?
(B) Is there any evidence at all against the claim that dinosaurs are closely related to birds?
(C) How likely is it for animals that are not closely related to each other to have similar collagen proteins?
(D) Is it possible that *T. rex* is more closely related to modern-day chickens than to certain other types of dinosaurs?
(E) Before Schweitzer's discovery, did researchers suppose that the collagen proteins in *T. rex* and chickens might be similar?

11. A university professor researching sleep disorders occasionally taught class after spending whole nights working in a laboratory. She found lecturing after such nights difficult: she reported that she felt worn out and humorless, and she had difficulty concentrating and finding the appropriate words. After several weeks of lectures, she asked her students to guess which lectures had been given after nights without sleep. Interestingly, very few students were able to correctly identify them.

Which one of the following statements is most strongly supported by the information above?

(A) The subjective effects of occasional sleep deprivation are more pronounced than are its effects on overt behavior.
(B) No one can assess the overall effects of sleep deprivation on a particular person as well as that sleep-deprived person can.
(C) Sleep deprivation has less effect on professors' job performance than it does on the job performance of others.
(D) Occasional sleep deprivation is not as debilitating as extended sleep deprivation.
(E) University students in a lecture audience tend to be astute observers of human behavior.

GO ON TO THE NEXT PAGE.

12. Prime minister: Our nation's government should give priority to satisfying the needs of our nation's people over satisfying the needs of people of any other nation. This is despite the fact that the people of other nations are equal in worth to the people of our nation, which means that it is objectively no more important to satisfy the needs of our nation's people than to satisfy those of other nations' people.

Which one of the following principles, if valid, most helps to reconcile the apparent conflict among the prime minister's claims?

(A) A nation's government should not attempt to satisfy the needs of a group of people unless the satisfaction of those people's needs is objectively more important than that of any other group's needs.

(B) A nation's government should give priority to satisfying the needs of its own people over satisfying the needs of another nation's people only if its own people are more worthy than the other nation's people.

(C) The priority a nation's government should place on satisfying the needs of a group of people depends mainly on how objectively important it is for the needs of those people to be satisfied.

(D) When the people of two nations are equally worthy, the needs of the people of each of those nations should be satisfied primarily by the people's own governments.

(E) A nation's government should give priority to the satisfaction of the needs of a group of people if, but only if, there is no other way for that group's needs to be satisfied.

13. Mayor: To keep our neighborhoods clean, every street in town will be swept at least once a month. If a neighborhood needs more frequent sweepings, due to excessive dirt from major construction for example, that neighborhood will be qualified for interim sweepings. All requests for interim sweepings from qualified neighborhoods will be satisfied immediately.

If all of the mayor's statements are true, then which one of the following must also be true?

(A) All neighborhoods in which construction is under way are qualified neighborhoods.

(B) All qualified neighborhoods will get their streets swept more than once a month.

(C) No street will be swept more than once a month unless it is located in a qualified neighborhood.

(D) A qualified neighborhood that requests an interim sweeping will have its streets swept more than once a month.

(E) No street in an unqualified neighborhood will be swept more than once a month even if the neighborhood requests it.

14. Journalist: It is unethical for journalists to lie—to say something untrue with the purpose of deceiving the listener—to get a story. However, journalists commonly withhold relevant information in interviews in order to elicit new information. Some argue that this, like lying, is intentional deception and therefore unethical. However, this argument fails to recognize the distinction between failing to prevent a false belief and actively encouraging one. Lying is unethical because it actively encourages a false belief.

The journalist argues by

(A) pointing out a difference between the two cases being compared in order to show that a conclusion based on their similarities should not be drawn

(B) defending what the journalist considers a controversial distinction by offering an example of a clear instance of it

(C) defining a concept and then showing that under this definition the concept applies to all of the cases under discussion

(D) appealing to a counterexample to undermine an ethical principle that supports an argument the journalist is trying to refute

(E) clarifying and defending a moral principle by comparing a case in which it applies to one in which it does not apply

15. Economist: Many of my colleagues are arguing that interest rates should be further lowered in order to stimulate economic growth. However, no such stimulation is needed: the economy is already growing at a sustainable rate. So, currently there is no reason to lower interest rates further.

The reasoning in the economist's argument is questionable in that the argument

(A) relies solely on the testimony of experts

(B) confuses economic growth with what stimulates it

(C) presumes that a need to stimulate economic growth is the only possible reason to lower interest rates now

(D) takes what is merely one way of stimulating economic growth to be the only way of stimulating economic growth

(E) concludes that a further reduction of interest rates would lead to unsustainable economic growth merely from the fact that the economy is already growing at a sustainable rate

GO ON TO THE NEXT PAGE.

16. Most commentators on Baroque painting consider Caravaggio an early practitioner of that style, believing that his realism and novel use of the interplay of light and shadow broke sharply with current styles of Caravaggio's time and significantly influenced seventeenth-century Baroque painting. One must therefore either abandon the opinion of this majority of commentators or reject Mather's definition of Baroque painting, which says that for any painting to be considered Baroque, it must display opulence, heroic sweep, and extravagance.

The conclusion of the argument can be properly drawn if which one of the following is assumed?

(A)   Paintings that belong to a single historical period typically share many of the same stylistic features.
(B)   A painter who makes use of the interplay of light and shadow need not for that reason be considered a nonrealistic painter.
(C)   Realism was not widely used by painters prior to the seventeenth century.
(D)   A realistic painting usually does not depict the world as opulent, heroic, or extravagant.
(E)   Opulence, heroic sweep, and extravagance are not present in Caravaggio's paintings.

17. Under the legal doctrine of jury nullification, a jury may legitimately acquit a defendant it believes violated a law if the jury believes that law to be unjust. Proponents argue that this practice is legitimate because it helps shield against injustice. But the doctrine relies excessively on jurors' objectivity. When juries are empowered to acquit on grounds of their perceptions of unfairness, they too often make serious mistakes.

The argument uses which one of the following techniques in its attempt to undermine the position that it attributes to the proponents of jury nullification?

(A)   attacking the motives of the proponents of the doctrine
(B)   identifying an inconsistency within the reasoning used to support the position
(C)   attempting to show that a premise put forward in support of the position is false
(D)   presenting a purported counterexample to a general claim made by the doctrine's proponents
(E)   arguing that the application of the doctrine has undesirable consequences

18. Pharmacist: A large study of people aged 65–81 and suffering from insomnia showed that most of insomnia's symptoms are substantially alleviated by ingesting melatonin, a hormone produced by the pineal gland, which plays a role in the regulation of the body's biological clock. Thus, the recent claims made by manufacturers of melatonin supplements that the pineal gland produces less melatonin as it ages are evidently correct.

The pharmacist's argument is flawed in that it

(A)   infers from the effect of an action that the action is intended to produce that effect
(B)   relies on the opinions of individuals who are likely to be biased
(C)   depends on using two different meanings for the same term to draw its conclusion
(D)   confuses an effect of a phenomenon with its cause
(E)   relies on a sample that is unrepresentative

GO ON TO THE NEXT PAGE.

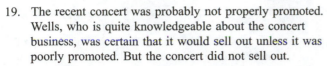

19. The recent concert was probably not properly promoted. Wells, who is quite knowledgeable about the concert business, was certain that it would sell out unless it was poorly promoted. But the concert did not sell out.

The pattern of reasoning in which one of the following is most similar to that in the argument above?

(A) Dr. Smith, a well-trained cardiologist, said the patient would probably survive the heart transplant if it were performed by a highly skilled surgeon. Thus, since the patient did not survive the surgery, it probably was not properly performed.

(B) Professor Willis, who is quite knowledgeable about organic chemistry, said that the sample probably did not contain any organic compounds. So, the sample probably is not labeled correctly, for if it were, it would contain organic compounds.

(C) My neighbor, who is an experienced home renovator, said the damage to the wall would not be noticeable if it were properly repaired. Thus, the repair to the wall probably was not properly done, since one can still notice the damage.

(D) The builder said that the school's roof would not require repairs for years, unless it is damaged in a storm. The roof is already leaking. Thus, since there have been no major storms, the builder was probably wrong.

(E) Professor Yanakita, who is an expert on the subject, said that the tests would find lead in the soil if they were properly conducted. So, since the tests did find lead in the soil, they probably were properly conducted.

20. Economist: Global recessions can never be prevented, for they could be prevented only if they were predictable. Yet economists, using the best techniques at their disposal, consistently fail to accurately predict global recessions.

The economist's argument is most vulnerable to the criticism that it

(A) presupposes in a premise the conclusion that it purports to establish

(B) fails to establish that economists claim to be able to accurately predict global recessions

(C) treats the predictability of an event, which is required for the event to be preventable, as a characteristic that assures its prevention

(D) fails to address the possibility that the techniques available to economists for the prediction of global recessions will significantly improve

(E) implicitly bases an inference that something will not occur solely on the information that its occurrence is not predictable

21. Letter to the editor: When your newspaper reported the (admittedly extraordinary) claim by Mr. Hanlon that he saw an alien spaceship, the tone of your article was very skeptical despite the fact that Hanlon has over the years proved to be a trusted member of the community. If Hanlon claimed to have observed a rare natural phenomenon like a large meteor, your article would not have been skeptical. So your newspaper exhibits an unjustified bias.

The argument in the letter conflicts with which one of the following principles?

(A) If a claim is extraordinary, it should not be presented uncritically unless it is backed by evidence of an extraordinarily high standard.

(B) One should be skeptical of claims that are based upon testimonial evidence that is acquired only through an intermediary source.

(C) If a media outlet has trusted a source in the past and the source has a good reputation, the outlet should continue to trust that source.

(D) People who think they observe supernatural phenomena should not publicize that fact unless they can present corroborating evidence.

(E) A newspaper should not publish a report unless it is confirmed by an independent source.

22. Fish with teeth specialized for scraping algae occur in both Flower Lake and Blue Lake. Some biologists argue that because such specialized characteristics are rare, fish species that have them should be expected to be closely related. If they are closely related, then the algae-scraping specialization evolved only once. But genetic tests show that the two algae-scraping species, although possibly related, are not closely related. Thus, the algae-scraping specialization evolved more than once.

The reasoning in the argument is flawed in that it

(A) infers a cause merely from a correlation

(B) infers that just because the evidence for a particular claim has not yet been confirmed, that claim is false

(C) takes a sufficient condition as a necessary one

(D) infers merely because something was likely to occur that it did occur

(E) appeals to the authority of biologists who may not be representative of all biologists with expertise in the relevant area

GO ON TO THE NEXT PAGE.

23. The constitution of Country F requires that whenever the government sells a state-owned entity, it must sell that entity for the highest price it can command on the open market. The constitution also requires that whenever the government sells a state-owned entity, it must ensure that citizens of Country F will have majority ownership of the resulting company for at least one year after the sale.

The government of Country F must violate at least one of the constitutional requirements described above if it is faced with which one of the following situations?

(A) The government will sell StateAir, a state-owned airline. The highest bid received was from a corporation that was owned entirely by citizens of Country F when the bid was received. Shortly after the bid was received, however, noncitizens purchased a minority share in the corporation.

(B) The government has agreed to sell National Silver, a state-owned mine, to a corporation. Although citizens of Country F have majority ownership of the corporation, most of the corporation's operations and sales take place in other countries.

(C) The government will sell PetroNat, a state-owned oil company. World Oil Company has made one of the highest offers for PetroNat, but World Oil's ownership structure is so complex that the government cannot determine whether citizens of Country F have majority ownership.

(D) The government will sell National Telephone, a state-owned utility. The highest bid received was from a company in which citizens of Country F have majority ownership but noncitizens own a minority share. However, the second-highest bid, from a consortium of investors all of whom are citizens of Country F, was almost as high as the highest bid.

(E) The government will sell StateRail, a state-owned railway. The government must place significant restrictions on who can purchase StateRail to ensure that citizens of Country F will gain majority ownership. However, any such restrictions will reduce the price the government receives for StateRail.

24. The makers of Activite, a natural dietary supplement, claim that it promotes energy and mental alertness. To back up their claim, they offer a month's supply of Activite free to new customers. Clearly, Activite must be effective, since otherwise it would not be in the company's interest to make such an offer.

Which one of the following, if true, most weakens the argument?

(A) The nutrients in Activite can all be obtained from a sufficiently varied and well-balanced diet.

(B) There are less expensive dietary supplements on the market that are just as effective as Activite.

(C) A month is not a sufficient length of time for most dietary supplements to be fully effective.

(D) The makers of Activite charge a handling fee that is considerably more than what it costs them to pack and ship their product.

(E) The mere fact that a dietary supplement contains only natural ingredients does not insure that it has no harmful side effects.

GO ON TO THE NEXT PAGE.

25. Of the citizens who disapprove of the prime minister's overall job performance, most disapprove because of the prime minister's support for increasing the income tax. However, Theresa believes that the income tax should be increased. So Theresa probably approves of the prime minister's overall job performance.

Which one of the following arguments exhibits flawed reasoning that is most parallel to that in the argument above?

(A) Of the people who support allowing limited logging in the Grizzly National Forest, most support it because they think it will reduce the risk of fire in the forest. Andy thinks that limited logging will not reduce the risk of fire in the forest, so he probably opposes allowing limited logging there.

(B) Of the people who expect the population in the area to increase over the next ten years, most think that an expected population increase is a good reason to build a new school. Bonita does not expect the population to increase over the next ten years, so she probably does not favor building a new school.

(C) Of the people who believe that the overall economy has improved, most believe it because they believe that their own financial situation has improved. Chung believes that the economy has worsened, so he probably believes that his own financial situation has worsened.

(D) Of the people who oppose funding a study to determine the feasibility of building a light rail line in the Loffoch Valley, most also believe that the Valley Freeway should be built. Donna opposes increasing funding for a study, so she probably supports building the Valley Freeway.

(E) Of the people who believe that there will be a blizzard tomorrow, most believe it because of the weather report on the Channel 9 news. Eduardo believes that there will be a blizzard tomorrow, so he probably saw the weather report on the Channel 9 news.

26. Bird watcher: The decrease in the mourning-dove population in this area is probably a result of the loss of nesting habitat. Many mourning doves had formerly nested in the nearby orchards, but after overhead sprinklers were installed in the orchards last year, the doves ceased building nests there.

Which one of the following, if true, most strengthens the argument?

(A) Mourning doves were recently designated a migratory game species, meaning that they can be legally hunted.

(B) The trees in the nearby orchards were the only type of trees in the area attractive to nesting mourning doves.

(C) Blue jays that had nested in the orchards also ceased doing so after the sprinklers were installed.

(D) Many residents of the area fill their bird feeders with canola or wheat, which are appropriate seeds for attracting mourning doves.

(E) Mourning doves often nest in fruit trees.

S T O P

IF YOU FINISH BEFORE TIME IS CALLED, YOU MAY CHECK YOUR WORK ON THIS SECTION ONLY.
DO NOT WORK ON ANY OTHER SECTION IN THE TEST.

Acknowledgment is made to the following sources from which material has been adapted for use in this test booklet:

Michael S. Gazzaniga and Megan S. Steven, "Neuroscience and the Law." ©2007 by Scientific American, Inc. http://www.sciammind.com/article.cfm?articleID=00053249-43D1-123A-822283414B7F4945.

Jeffrey Rosen, "The Brain on the Stand." ©2007 by The New York Times Company. http://www.nytimes.com/2007/03/11/magazine/11Neurolaw.t.html?_r=2&oref=slogin&oref=slogin.

Angus Trumble, "Smelly Masterpieces." ©2008 by Times Newspapers Ltd.

Kipling D. Williams, Martin J. Bourgeois, and Robert T. Croyle, "The Effects of Stealing Thunder in Criminal and Civil Trials." ©1993 by Plenum Publishing Corporation.

Wait for the supervisor's instructions before you open the page to the topic.
Please print and sign your name and write the date in the designated spaces below.

Time: 35 Minutes

General Directions

You will have 35 minutes in which to plan and write an essay on the topic inside. Read the topic and the accompanying directions carefully. You will probably find it best to spend a few minutes considering the topic and organizing your thoughts before you begin writing. In your essay, be sure to develop your ideas fully, leaving time, if possible, to review what you have written. **Do not write on a topic other than the one specified. Writing on a topic of your own choice is not acceptable.**

No special knowledge is required or expected for this writing exercise. Law schools are interested in the reasoning, clarity, organization, language usage, and writing mechanics displayed in your essay. How well you write is more important than how much you write.

Confine your essay to the blocked, lined area on the front and back of the separate Writing Sample Response Sheet. Only that area will be reproduced for law schools. Be sure that your writing is legible.

Both this topic sheet and your response sheet must be turned in to the testing staff before you leave the room.

Topic Code
126351

Date
/ /

Print Your Full Name Here		
Last	First	M.I.

Sign Your Name Here

LSAT® Writing Sample Topic

Directions: The scenario presented below describes two choices, either one of which can be supported on the basis of the information given. Your essay should consider both choices and argue for one over the other, based on the two specified criteria and the facts provided. There is no "right" or "wrong" choice: a reasonable argument can be made for either.

A brother and sister, Hector and Teresa, are deciding whether to spend the upcoming summer recording music and playing in cafes and bars together, or to continue in the summer along their original career paths. Using the facts below, write an essay in which you argue for one option over the other based on the following two criteria:

- They want the risks they take in their lives to reflect the potential rewards.
- They want to be responsible with respect to their educational preparation and the choices they have already made.

Hector and Teresa each have extensive musical training. They are talented enough that if they spend the summer on music, there is a good chance that they will become popular enough to get steady work performing and selling albums. It is unlikely that they will have another occasion to spend so much time together. Spending the summer on music could allow them to develop their sibling relationship, which has not been very close because of their five-year age difference. Spending so much time together could reveal personality clashes.

Teresa is pursuing her PhD in economics. She completed all the coursework and general examinations four years ago. Spending the summer on music might delay finishing her dissertation. This could further jeopardize her job prospects in a field where the opportunities have been diminishing. Hector has been working in a medical laboratory since receiving his undergraduate degree five years ago. To advance in his field, he is scheduled to begin a difficult master's program in biochemistry early in the fall. Hector and Teresa each might have to go into debt as a consequence of spending the summer on music.

WP-V126

Scratch Paper
Do not write your essay in this space.

COMPUTING YOUR SCORE

Directions:

1. Use the Answer Key on the next page to check your answers.

2. Use the Scoring Worksheet below to compute your raw score.

3. Use the Score Conversion Chart to convert your raw score into the 120–180 scale.

Scoring Worksheet

1. Enter the number of questions you answered correctly in each section.

	Number Correct
SECTION I..................	_____
SECTION II................	_____
SECTION III..............	_____
SECTION IV	_____

2. Enter the sum here: _____

   This is your Raw Score.

Conversion Chart
For Converting Raw Score to the 120–180 LSAT Scaled Score
LSAT Form 4LSN111

Reported Score	Raw Score Lowest	Raw Score Highest
180	99	101
179	98	98
178	97	97
177	96	96
176	95	95
175	*	*
174	94	94
173	93	93
172	92	92
171	90	91
170	89	89
169	88	88
168	86	87
167	85	85
166	84	84
165	82	83
164	80	81
163	79	79
162	77	78
161	75	76
160	74	74
159	72	73
158	70	71
157	68	69
156	67	67
155	65	66
154	63	64
153	61	62
152	59	60
151	58	58
150	56	57
149	54	55
148	53	53
147	51	52
146	49	50
145	48	48
144	46	47
143	44	45
142	43	43
141	41	42
140	40	40
139	38	39
138	36	37
137	35	35
136	33	34
135	32	32
134	31	31
133	29	30
132	28	28
131	27	27
130	25	26
129	24	24
128	23	23
127	22	22
126	21	21
125	20	20
124	19	19
123	18	18
122	17	17
121	16	16
120	0	15

*There is no raw score that will produce this scaled score for this form.

SECTION I

1.	C	8.	A	15.	E	22.	E
2.	C	9.	E	16.	D	23.	D
3.	B	10.	E	17.	A	24.	B
4.	C	11.	D	18.	A	25.	D
5.	C	12.	E	19.	A		
6.	A	13.	A	20.	E		
7.	E	14.	D	21.	B		

SECTION II

1.	C	8.	E	15.	B	22.	B
2.	D	9.	A	16.	A	23.	C
3.	E	10.	A	17.	E		
4.	A	11.	A	18.	D		
5.	E	12.	C	19.	B		
6.	E	13.	E	20.	B		
7.	B	14.	D	21.	A		

SECTION III

1.	D	8.	D	15.	A	22.	E
2.	E	9.	C	16.	D	23.	A
3.	A	10.	B	17.	B	24.	B
4.	A	11.	D	18.	A	25.	B
5.	B	12.	A	19.	B	26.	D
6.	B	13.	D	20.	C	27.	E
7.	B	14.	E	21.	C		

SECTION IV

1.	B	8.	B	15.	C	22.	C
2.	C	9.	B	16.	E	23.	E
3.	E	10.	C	17.	E	24.	D
4.	D	11.	A	18.	E	25.	A
5.	D	12.	D	19.	C	26.	B
6.	B	13.	D	20.	D		
7.	A	14.	A	21.	A		

LSAT® PREP TOOLS

NEW
10 Actual, Official LSAT PrepTests, Volume V™
(PrepTests 62–71)

It takes three years to produce enough PrepTests for a new 10 Actuals book! We are pleased to offer the latest in our 10 Actuals series: 10 Actual, Official LSAT PrepTests, Volume V. This new book is only the second in our 10 Actuals series to include previously administered Comparative Reading questions, which first appeared in the LSAT in 2007. This essential LSAT preparation tool encompasses PrepTest 62 (the December 2010 LSAT) through PrepTest 71 (the December 2013 LSAT).

For pure practice at an unbelievable price, you can't beat the 10 Actuals series. Each book includes:

• 10 previously administered LSATs
• an answer key for each test
• a writing sample for each test
• score-conversion tables

For the best value, purchase The Whole Test Prep Package V™, which includes the 10 Actual, Official LSAT PrepTests, Volume V, along with The Official LSAT SuperPrep® for only $38 (online only).

$24 Online

LSAC.org